THE EROTICA
ANTHOLOGY

THE EPICURE'S ANTHOLOGY

collected by
NANCY QUENNELL

with an essay on
The Epicure and the Epicurean
by
A.J.A. SYMONS
decorations by
OSBERT LANCASTER

Robin Clark
London

First published by Christopher and Anthony Sandford &
Owen Rutter in 1936 at The Golden Cockerel Press, London
First published in paperback by Robin Clark Limited 1991
A member of the Namara Group
27/29 Goodge Street, London W1P 1FD

Anthology copyright © by John Fielden 1978, 1991

This book is sold subject to the condition that it shall not, by way of
trade or otherwise, be lent, sold, hired out, or otherwise circulated
without the Publisher's prior consent in any form of binding or cover
other than that in which it is published and without a similar
condition including this condition being imposed on the subsequent
purchaser. This book is published at a net price and is supplied
subject to the Publishers Association Standard Conditions of Sale
registered under the Restrictive Trades Practices Act, 1956.

British Library Cataloguing in Publication Data

The epicure's anthology
I. Quennell, Nancy
820.8
ISBN 0 86072 137 X

Printed and bound in Great Britain by
Cox & Wyman, Reading, Berks, England

TO
JACK FIELDEN
who understands the art of dining

ACKNOWLEDGEMENTS

My thanks are due to John Hayward and John Grey Murray, for advice and help: and to Lady Gollancz, Edith Sitwell, Arthur Waley and Powys Mathers, for kind permission to use selections from their books: also to Messrs. Jonathan Cape, Duckworth, Macmillan, Chatto and Windus, Faber and Faber, and Heinemann.

N. Q.

CONTENTS OF THE ANTHOLOGY

I: BANQUETING DELIGHTS

	Page
A CARTHAGINIAN FEAST Flaubert, *Salambo* (trans: by Powys Mathers)	27
TRIMALCHIO'S FEAST Petronius, *The Satyricon* (trans: by Burnaby)	29
JORROCKS IN FRANCE Surtees, *Jorrocks's Jaunts*	35
A ROMAN BANQUET Smollett, *Peregrine Pickle*	39
A CHRISTMAS DINNER Dickens, *A Christmas Carol*	43
DR. FOLLIOTT AT DINNER Peacock, *Crochet Castle*	45
THOMAS WALKER'S WHITEBAIT DINNER Walker, *The Original*	47
LUNCH AT COMBRAY Proust, *Swann's Way* (trans: by Scott Moncrieff)	48
EASTER SUNDAY WITH JOHNSON Boswell, *Life of Samuel Johnson*	50
A FEAST IN PARADISE Milton, *Paradise Lost*	51

II: REPAS GALANTS

A WHITE DINNER Thackeray, *Pendennis*	55

	Page
TOM JONES CAPTIVATED Fielding, *Tom Jones*	57
A RENDEZVOUS IN A BATH Boccaccio, *The Decameron*	60
AN APHRODISIAC DIET Burton, *The Anatomy of Melancholy*	63
A BANQUET Boccaccio, *The Decameron*	64
THE PREPARATION OF VENUS Apuleius, *The Golden Asse* (trans: by Adlington)	66
BECKY SETS HER CAP AT A RICH ANGLO-INDIAN Thackeray, *Vanity Fair*	67
ULYSSES ENTERTAINED BY CIRCE Homer, *The Odyssey* (trans: by Samuel Butler)	69
FROM THE SONG OF SONGS *Holy Bible* (Authorised Version)	71
FEAST OF ST. AGNES Keats, *The Eve of St. Agnes*	72
LA POULARDE DE BRESSE Brillat-Savarin, *La Physiologie du Goût*	74
THE NUPTIAL FEAST OF JANUARY AND MAY Pope, *January and May*	76
VÉNUS AURA SON TOUR Andréa de Nerçiat, *Contes Nouveaux*	78
THE FOOD OF LOVE Mrs. Leyel, *The Magic of Herbs*	79

III: THE PHILOSOPHY OF FOOD

CHARACTERISTICS OF THE GOURMET
Brillat-Savarin, *La Physiologie du Goût* — 85

'DOTH A MAN THAT IS ADRY DESIRE TO DRINK IN GOLD?'
Burton, *Anatomy of Melancholy* — 86

GOURMANDISE
Brillat-Savarin, *La Physiologie du Goût* — 87

'HE DINES UNSCATHED WHO DINES ALONE'
The Letters of Madame du Deffand to Horace Walpole — 89

JUVENAL'S FIFTH SATIRE
Juvenal, *Satires* (trans: by Gifford) — 90

DELICATE HUMANITY
Boswell, *Life of Samuel Johnson* — 93

A GREAT AND GOOD MAN
Sanders, *The Holland House Circle* — 94

'GOD HELP THE WICKED'
Rochester-Savile Correspondance — 95

A GOOD APPETITE THE BEST SAUCE
Pope, *Imitations of the Satires of Horace* — 96

IV: GASTRONOMIC ODDITIES

DESSERT
Lord Orford, *Works* — 101

LES FANTAISIES GASTRONOMIQUES DE LUNÉVILLE
Maugras, *La Cour de Lunéville au XVIIIme Siècle* — 102

ROMAN LUXURIES
Apician Morsels. Anon. — 104

GOOD HOUSEKEEPING—in 1665
May, *The Accomplish'd Cook* — 106

'TO IMITATE IN SUCH A MANNER IS TO CREATE'
Soyer, *Pantropheon* — 107

NAPOLEON'S COOKS
Disraeli, *Tancred* — 108

FOIE GRAS
Lord Lytton, *Pelham* — 109

GASTRONOMIC ECCENTRICITIES
Soyer, *Pantropheon* — 110

A MODEST PROPOSAL
Swift, *A Modest Proposal* — 114

THACKERAY ON SWIFT'S PROPOSAL
Thackeray, *The Four Georges* — 117

TO COLERIDGE
Lamb, *Letters* — 118

A DAINTY ASSE
Apuleius, *The Golden Asse* (trans: by Adlington) — 119

A BROKEN ENGAGEMENT
Jane Austen, *Lesley Castle* — 121

VEAL PIE
Dickens, *Pickwick Papers* — 123

A RECTORY BREAKFAST	Page
Trollope, *The Warden*	124
THE OYSTERS	
Thackeray, *Fitz-boodle's Confessions*	126

V: FESTIVE SCENES

BEING A PART OF THE ENTERTAINMENT UNTO QUEEN ELIZABETH AT THE CASTLE OF KENILWORTH IN 1575	
Robert Laneham's Letter (Edited by Furnivall)	133
DINNER AT THE ROTHSCHILDS'	
Lady Morgan, *Letters*	135
A PICNIC IN WESTMINSTER ABBEY	
Hickey, *Memoirs*	137
SUPPER IN A GROTTO AT STOWE	
The Letters of Madame du Deffand to Horace Walpole	139
FASHIONABLE LONDON AT THE TIME OF SWIFT, ADDISON, AND STEELE	
Thackeray, *The Four Georges*	141
A FOURTEENTH CENTURY BANQUET	
Winner and Waster (ed: by Gollancz)	144
AN ENGLISH AND A CHINESE DINNER	
Hickey, *Memoirs*	145
A BANQUET AT STRAWBERRY HILL	
Melville, *Horace Walpole*	146
EXTRACTS FROM MISS BERRY'S JOURNAL: 1802	
The Journals and Correspondence of Miss Berry	147

DINNER WITH THE ABBOT OF ALCO-
    BACA   *Page*
Travel Diaries of William Beckford   151

A RECEPTION AT GENJI'S PALACE
Lady Murasaki, *Blue Trousers* (trans: by Waley)   153

FAME
Disraeli, *Lothair*   155

ENTREMETS
Soyer, *Pantropheon*   157

A FÊTE FOR THE DUKE OF WELLING-
    TON
Fulford, *George IV*   158

REGENCY FÊTES
Fulford, *George IV*   159

A MOSCOW DINNER: 1804
*The Russian Journals of Martha and Catherine
    Wilmot* (Edited by Lady Londonderry)   163

A TRAINEAU PARTY
*The Russian Journals of Martha and Catherine
    Wilmot* (Edited by Lady Londonderry)   165

COFFEE IN A BAGNIO IN ADRIANOPLE
Lady Mary Wortley-Montague, *Letters*   166

LA FÊTE DE VERSAILLES
Anon, 1668   168

VI: GASTRONOMIC INCIDENTS

A GREAT EPICURE
Gronow, *Reminiscences*   173

'A PEACOCKE IS GREATER THAN AN
   APPLE'   *Page*
Apician Morsels. Anon.   174

DES HUÎTRES TOUS LES MATINS
Saint-Evrémont, *Letter to Mlle. de Lanclos*   175

VATEL'S TRAGEDY
Madame de Sevigné, *Letters*   176

TRUFFES À LA PURÉE
The Art of Dining. Anon.   178

A CHEF
The Art of Dining. Anon.   179

AN ANECDOTE
The Art of Dining. Anon.   180

A BET
Boswell, *Life of Samuel Johnson*   181

THE LION'S SHARE
Edith Sitwell, *The English Eccentrics*   182

BYRON'S DINNER WITH ROGERS
Rogers, *Table-Talk*   184

AN ECONOMICAL DINNER
J. T. Smith, *Nollekens and his Times*   185

JOHNSON ON THE FRENCH
Boswell, *Life of Samuel Johnson*   187

SWIFT'S HOSPITALITY
Edith Sitwell, *Alexander Pope*   188

NOTE ON THE ANTHOLOGY

MAN, embroidering on the primitive act of eating, has eventually created a comprehensive function, a ceremony significant in a variety of ways, illustrative of culture or decadence and so revealing that the table metamorphosed becomes a stage on which both poets and emperors appear, the scene of endless productions, many of them magnificently spectacular, whilst others are remarkable less for their décor than for characterisation and brilliance of dialogue; and some are curious and fantastic experiments designed to stimulate a jaded audience; the remainder, *drames amoureuses*, idyllic embarkations for Cytherea...

Thus 'all the world's a stage,' and the *table*, besides providing exits and entrances, supplies a very valuable key to the history of Civilisation ... a reflection which gave rise to the following anthology, in which have been collected some examples of the various kinds of gastronomic drama. No endeavour has been made to make it comprehensive. Where a choice was to be made between subjects suggestive of a similar theme, often the least well-known has been selected. In view of the preference of many people for reading extracts from French literature untranslated, while good translations are in fact available, a few have been left in the original.

N.Q.

THE EPICURE AND THE EPICUREAN

GASTRONOMY is one of those pleasures that have allied themselves to literature, and therefore are remembered. Many phases of life in classical days have vanished from our knowledge; many of the minutiæ of the middle ages can only be surmised; and the record of affairs even as conducted by the Victorians is in some ways already obscure or imperfect. But we know how almost every people of the past, near or remote, has eaten and drunk. What sauces the Greeks used, how the Romans stewed their dormice, what names were given by the Norman conquerors to the divisions and subdivisions of the beasts of the chase, what parts of the human body were preferred by the Congo cannibals, are questions which belong, not to the domain of conjecture, but to that of verified knowledge. We know (at least, those who care to *can* know) what fare was set before the unjust lords of the Star Chamber, how the court of Louis XIV was fed, what, and even where, Nelson, Wellington and Marlborough ate. 'I dined to-day with your Mr. Sterne by invitation and drank Irish wine,' wrote Swift to Stella, and we know what he meant. 'I dined again yesterday at Blackwall as a guest, and observed that my theory as to adjuncts was carefully put into practice,' remarks Thomas Walker, and we know what the theory was. And, though he said nothing aloud, we know what Professor Saintsbury said to himself when his twelve guests, who had all refused an excellent soufflé, changed their minds one by one when the Professor, to whom it was served last, helped himself. We have his own authority: he said 'Sheep.'

But, despite this vast accumulation of gastronomic

detail and knowledge, in which there is material for a whole library of anthologies, we are still strangely ill-informed concerning the epicure himself. He has been accepted rather than defined; and though, as a type, he is perpetual, and renewed in every generation, his appearances in fiction are few and unsatisfactory. Even to this day the associations that are thought to cling to his character make him, in England at least, an unpopular figure, subject to disapproval and distrust. To confess oneself an epicure is to invite a tinge of that suspicion which has for so long attached itself to the Epicurean. Is it a survival of our Puritanism that the English terms for the table-lover are both contemptuous: glutton and gorbelly? Dr. Johnson admitted to his dictionary another unfavourable term, 'gormand': it is typical that he did not include 'gourmet.' 'Epicure' he defined as 'a man given wholly to luxury.'

Modern usage, however, recognises a distinction between the epicure and the Epicurean—a distinction which must be emphasised if the former is ever to be freed from the reproach that shadows his name. Originally the two words were merely variants of one term describing a follower of Epicurus (320–270 B.C.), a believer in his teachings. But, in the strictest sense, its use in that connection was short-lived, since the disciples of Epicurus very early reversed his doctrines by exaggerating one part and abandoning another. Epicurus taught that pleasure is the supreme good, the end of life; but he taught also that pleasure consists in serenity of mind and absence of pain, and can best be obtained by the man who is ready to reject dangerous or disturbing gratifications in favour of permanent and tranquil well-being. In effect he asserted that not only is pleasure the only good, but also that good is the only source of pleasure. He was an apostle of moderation, and, as might be expected, his moderation did not commend itself to his followers, who, though they knew their own desires well enough, could not tell which pleasures were likely to carry a sting in their tail—or, when they could tell, were prepared to take the risk. Their reversed doctrine proved far more acceptable than the austere original. Men distrust moderation. 'The golden mean is that there is no golden mean'; and pleasures which are recommended by lack of penalty pale before those which are positive and supreme in their own moments. Gradually the name of Epicurus became attached to a philosophic system he had never promoted, and an attitude to life which he denied. In the seventeenth century St. Evremond and Cowley, among others, made vain efforts to restore his name to the teachings truly his, but failed, and the false associations of the word 'Epicurean' remained current and universal.

For centuries the imaginary figure of the epicurean, consciously devoting his life to the pursuit of pleasure, bending all his powers to that end, has attracted and repelled the Western mind. 'Every age of European thought has had its Cyrenaics or Epicureans, under many disguises, even under the hood of the monk" observes Pater. Faust is one of the many figures in whom the pleasure-seeker is personified; but what he seeks is shown as being procurable only at the price of damnation, at the cost of himself, of his soul. Bradley has summarised the general answer: 'Common opinion repeats its old song, that the search for pleasure is the coarsest form of vulgar delusion, that if you want to be happy in the sense of being pleased, you must not think of pleasure, but, taking up some accredited form of living, must make that your end, and in that case, with moderately good fortune, you will be happy.'

Although there can be no final answer to such questions, it is clear that the man who makes pleasure his sole principle must face the distrust, if also the envy, of the world. And it is in this distrust, this denial, that the opposition to the epicure is wrongly rooted. He falls under the same ban as the epicurean. But the ban is unjust, for the two characters seek different goals. The epicurean is a sceptic who values nothing save his own sensations, and suborns his intelligence to the unending task of refining and intensifying them; whereas the epicure is, or at least may be, a man of faith who affirms and enjoys the gastronomic pleasures as a justification of life.

The epicure is most frequently a man of affairs, who has distinguished himself by talent, or played some prominent part in the world's administration, to whom care in eating and drinking is a relaxation, a hobby, or an inspiration. The modern definition 'one who cultivates a refined taste for the pleasures of the table' is explicit & sufficient; and no qualification should be added to it. The epicure is not a man who thinks of, and lives for, his belly alone; he is not a sensualist for whom dinner is merely an elaborate prelude to sexual passion; he is not a hedonist who sees life as a succession of pleasurable sensations to be obtained by hook, crook, or levitation; he is not a table-bore who rams his one subject down your throat; he is not a pride-starved victim of insufficiency striving to assert a false superiority by making undue fuss over wine and food. He is simply 'one who cultivates a refined taste for the pleasures of the table.' No more. He may profess any of a dozen religions (though not those of Mahomet or Confucius, which forbid wine), he may be a carpenter in Surrey or a Burgundy cooper, a colonel of infantry or a private detective; all that we can predict or expect of him is that, as an epicure, he conforms to the definition already quoted.

Indeed, instead of suspecting and distrusting the epicure, we should revere him. His attention to what he eats and drinks is the demand that encourages good cooks; and the dishes that his palate appreciates and creates pass from his table to those of countless others who are unaware of their benefactor. High among philanthropists, the devotee of an absorbing and harmless faith, he deserves our appreciation as one of the few enthusiasts whose hobby can have no evil effect either upon himself or on others.

Against Faust let us set the sturdy figure of George Saintsbury, certainly one of the half dozen most notable epicures in the English scene, who enshrined the memory of his cellar in discerning and expressive prose twenty years after he had ceased to drink wine, telling over again, bottle by bottle almost, and with a scholar's patience and care, the vanished contents of his empty bins. No one acquainted with Saintsbury's life and work can doubt that, so far from losing his soul, his character was benefited and his life enriched, by his gastronomic zeal. Instances might be multiplied, by the score, of distinguished men whose appreciation of the pleasures of the table has not been inconsistent with a life of worth and work. Whistler, Rossini, Lamb, Thackeray, Keats rush at once to the mind. Brillat-Savarin, the supreme epicure, asserted the four strongholds of his favourite study to be letters, the church, medicine and finance—to which surely, by his own example, we must add law. That general opinion which, according to Bradley, has decided against the epicurean, would, if it could judge the issue fairly, accept the pastime of the epicure as one of the most reasonable & beneficent elements in human existence.

The present anthology has been drawn from the works and correspondence of many minds. Any selection from a field so vast must of necessity omit numerous particular pieces which the reader, were he editor, would include; and it is therefore personal regret, rather than adverse criticism, to note the absence of any entries from Saintsbury's *Notes on a Cellar Book*, that enthralling work which has led to a dining club being founded in honour of its author; or of any extracts from the scattered culinary writings of George Augustus Sala, that forgotten epicure who wrote in rococo-Victorian sentences as characteristic of their period as is the Crystal Palace, and was familiar at first hand with the cooking of every country in Europe; or of any sample from the rich mines of our modern St. Evremond, Monsieur André Simon, who pays us the compliment of writing his entrancing works in English. And in the gallery of fictional epicures, let us wave a hand to the absent, magnificent Porthos du Vallon, whose appetitite enlivens so many pages of Dumas. Despite the size and comprehensiveness of his hunger, Porthos was a first-rate judge of wine and food, as he proved at the King's table; and his creator has endowed him with the true epicure's satisfaction after dining well—a satisfaction that makes its owner unapprehensive of dangers and indifferent to quotidian cares.

But regret for the missing Sala, Saintsbury and Porthos, need not affect our appreciation of these 'banqueting delights.' We do not all make the same choice from even the most tempting menu; nor can the hungriest of us attempt, at one sitting, all the dishes listed on a bill of fare. It is sufficient if we are given a variety of good things from which to select our own dinner. Mrs. Quennell has set before us many charming and instructive extracts gathered from the writings of widely different times and types; let us be grateful for all she gives us, and enjoy both the present feast and the prospect of other delicacies still untasted.

A. J. A. SYMONS.

I: BANQUETING DELIGHTS

Celui qui reçoit ses amis et ne donne aucun soin personnel au repas qui leur est préparé n'est pas digne d'avoir des amis.

BRILLAT-SAVARIN.

A CARTHAGINIAN FEAST

MEN OF ALL NATIONS were there, Ligurians and Lusitanians, Balearic Islanders, Negroes, and fugitives from Rome...

They lay upon cushions; they squatted around huge trays, and so ate; others, lying upon their bellies, reached out for lumps of meat and gorged themselves, leaning on their elbows in the placid posture of lions dismembering their prey. Late-comers, leaning against the trees, watched the low tables half hidden under their scarlet coverings, and awaited their turn.

Since Hamilcar's kitchens were inadequate, the Council had provided slaves, dishes and couches. Oxen were roasting at great clear fires in the middle of the garden, which thus looked like a battlefield when the dead are being burned. Loaves dusted with aniseed vied with huge cheeses heavier than disks, and great bowls of wine with mighty water tankards, set close to gold filigree baskets full of flowers. Their eyes gleamed wide in delight at being at last free to gorge to their hearts' content; and here and there they were beginning to sing.

First they were served with birds in green sauce upon plates of red clay, decorated in black relief; then with every kind of shell-fish that is found on the Punic coasts, with broths thickened with wheat, beans and barley, and with cumin-spiced snails upon yellow amber dishes.

After this the tables were loaded with meats: antelopes still with their horns, peacocks still with their feathers, whole sheep cooked in sweet wine, camels' and buffaloes' haunches, hedgehogs in garum sauce, fried grasshoppers, and pickled dormice. Great pieces of fat were floating amid saffron in bowls of Tamrapanni wood.

Everywhere was a lavish abundance of pickles, truffles, and asafœtida. There were pyramids of fruit tumbling upon honeycombs; and they had not forgotten to serve some of those silky-coated, red, fat-paunched little dogs, fattened on olive lees: a Carthaginian dish which was an abomination to other peoples. Their stomachs' greed was titillated by the excitement and wonder of such novel fare. The Gauls, with their long hair coiled upon the top of their heads, snatched at water-melons and lemons, and crunched them peel and all. Negroes who had never seen a crawfish, tore their faces on its red spines. The Greeks, who were smooth-shaven and whiter than marble, threw the leavings of their plates behind them; while herdsmen from Brutium, clad in wolf-skins, ate in silence, their faces buried in their plates.

Night fell. The awning over the cypress avenue was drawn back, and torches were brought.

FLAUBERT, *Salambo* (trans: by Powys Mathers).

TRIMALCHIO'S FEAST

IN THE PORCH stood the Porter in a Green Livery, girt about with a Cherry-coloured Girdle, garbling of Pease in a Silver Charger; and overhead hung a Golden Cage with a Magpye in it, which gave us an All Hail as we entered ...

Then came a sumptuous Antepast; for we were all seated, but only Trimalchio, for whom, after a new fashion, the chief Place was reserved. Besides that, as part of the Entertainment there was set by us a large Vessel of Metheglin, with a Pannier, in the one part of which were white olives, in the other black; two broad Platters covered the Vessel, ... and on them Dormice strewed over with Honey and Poppy: There were also piping-hot Sausages on a Silver Gridiron, and under that large Damsons, with the Kernels of Pomegranates ...

In the meantime while we were yet picking a Relish here and there, a Cupboard was brought in with a Basket, in which was a Hen Carved in wood, her wings, lying round and hollow, as sitting on Brood; when presently the Consort struck up, and two Servants fell a'searching the Straw under her, and taking out some Peahen's Eggs, distributed them among the Company: At this Trimalchio changing Countenance, 'I commanded my Friends,' said he, 'the Hen to be set with Peahen's Eggs; and so help me Hercules, I'm afraid they may be half Hatch't: however we'll try if they are yet Suppable'.

The thing we received was a kind of Shell of at least Six Pounds weight, made of Paste, and moulded into the Figure of an Egg, which we easily broke; and for my part, I was like to have thrown away my share; for it seemed to me to have a Chick in it; till hearing an old Guest of the Tables saying it was some good Bit or other, I searched further into it, and found a delicate fat Wheatear, in the middle of a well peppered Yoke; On this Trimalchio stopped his play for a while, and requiring the like for himself proclaimed If any of us would have any more Metheglin, he was at liberty to take it; when of a sudden the Musick gave the Sign, and the first Course was scrabled away by a Company of Singers and Dancers; but in the Rustle it happening that a Dish fell on the Floor, a Boy took it up, and Trimalchio taking notice of it, pluck't him by the Ears, and commanded him to throw it down again; on which the Groom of the Chamber came with a Broom and swept away the Silver Dish, with whatsoever else had fallen from the Table.

When presently came in two long-haired Blacks, with small Leather Bottles such as with which they strew Sand on the Stage, and gave us Wine to wash our Hands, but no one offered us Water. We all admiring the Finicalness of the Entertainment, 'Mars,' said he, 'is a lover of Justice, and therefore let every one have a Table to himself, for having more Elbow-room, these nasty stinking boys will be less troublesome to us'; and thereupon large double-Ear'd Vessels of Glass close Plaistered over, were brought up with Labels about their Necks, upon which was this Inscription:

OPIMIAN MUSCADINE OF AN HUNDRED YEARS OLD

... We drank and admired everything, when in came a Servant with a Silver Puppet, so jointed and put together that it turned every way; and being more than once thrown upon the Table, cast itself into several Figures; on which Trimalchio came out of his Poetry ...

The Applause we gave him, was followed with a Service, but respecting the place not so considerable as might have been expected; However, the Novelty of the thing drew every Man's Eye upon it; it was a large Charger, with the twelve Signs round it; upon every one of which the Master Cook had laid somewhat or other suitable to the Sign. Upon Aries, Chick-pease (a Pulse not unlike a Ram's-head); upon Taurus a piece of Beef; upon Gemini a pair of Pendulums and Kidneys; upon Cancer a Coronet; upon Leo an African Figg; upon Virgo a well-grown Boy; upon Libra a pair of Scales, in one of which was a Tart, in the other a Custard; upon Scorpio a Pilchard; upon Sagittari a Grey-hound; upon Capricorn a Lobster; upon Aquarius a Goose; upon Pisces two Mullets and in the middle a Plat of Herbs, cut out like a green turf, and over them a Honey-comb. During this, a lesser Black carried about Bread in a Silver Oven, and with a hideous Voice, forced a Bawdy Song from a Buffoon that stunk like Assa Foetida ...

Then the fourth Consort struck up; at which the waiters fell a Dancing and took off the upper part of the Charger, under which was a Dish of cramm'd Fowl and the hinder Paps of a Sow that had farrowed but a day before, well Powdered, and in the middle a Hare, stuck in with Finns of Fish in his side, that he looked like a Flying Horse; and on the sides of the Fish four little Images that spouted a relishing Sauce on some Fish that lay near them, all of them brought from the River Euripus ...

The Dish was by this time taken away and the Guests

grown merry with Wine ... at last other servants came in and spread Coverlets on the Beds, on which were Painted Nets, Men in Ambush with Hunting-Poles, and whatever appertained to Hunting; Nor could we yet tell what to make of it; when we heard a great cry without and a pack of Beagles came and ran round the Table, and after them a large Trey, on which was a Boar of the first Magnitude, with a Cap on his Head (such as Slaves at their making Free, had set on theirs in token of Liberties); on his Tusks hung two Wicker Baskets, the one full of Dates, the other of Almonds; and about him lay little Pigs of Marchpane, as if they were sucking; they signified a Sow had farrowed and hang there as presents for the Guests to carry away with them.

To the cutting up of this Boar, here came not he that had carried about the Fowl as before, but a Swinging Fellow with a two-handed Beard, Buskins on his Legs, and a short Embroidered Coat; who drawing his Wood-Knife, made a large hole in the Boar's Side, out of which flew a company of Blackbirds; Then Fowlers stood ready with their Engines and caught them in a trice as they fluttered about the Room: On which Trimalchio ordering to every Man his Bird, 'See,' said he, 'what kind of Acorns this Wild Boar fed on': When presently the Boys took off the Baskets and distributed the Dates and Almonds among the Guests ...

From this up rose Trimalchio, and went to the Close-Stool; we also being at liberty, without a Tyrant over us, fell to some Table-talk ...

The cloth being again taken away, upon the next Musick were brought in Three fat Hogs with Collars, and Bells, about their necks; and he that had the charge of them told us the one was Two years old, the other Three, and third full grown. I took it at first to be a Company of Tumblers, that the Hogs, as the manner is, were to have shown us some Tricks in a Ring, till Trimalchio breaking my expectations, 'Which of them,' said he, 'will ye have for Supper? For Cocks, Pheasants, and the like Trifles are but Country fare, but my Cooks have Coppers and will boil a Calf whole'. And therewith commanding a Cook to be called for, he prevented our Choice by ordering him to kill the largest...

Of a sudden the Roof gave a crack, and the whole Room shook: For my part I got on my feet, but all in confusion, for fear some Tumbler might drop on my head; the same also were the rest of the Guests; still gaping and expecting what new thing should come from the Clouds: when straight the main Beams opened, and a vast Circle was let down, all round which hung Golden Garlands, and Alabaster Pots of Sweet Ointments.

While we were required to take up these presents, I chanced to cast an eye upon the Table, where there lay a fresh service of Cheese-cakes and Tarts, and in the midst of them a lusty Rundlet, stuck round with all sorts of Apples, and Grapes, as they commonly draw that Figure.

We greedily reached our hands towards it, when of a sudden, a new Diversion gave us fresh Mirth; for all the Cheese-cakes, Apples, and Tarts, upon the least touch, threw out a delicious liquid Perfume which fell upon us...

This held a while till Trimalchio calling for a second Service to entertain his new guests, the Servants took away the Tables that were before us, and having brought others, strewed the Room with Pin-dust, mixt with

Vermillion and Saffron. And what I never saw before, the dust of a looking-glass ground to Powder...

On which a spruce Boy that served us with warm Water began to imitate a Nightingale; till Trimalchio giving the word, a Servant that waited on Habinas set up another Humour...

Nor had there ever been an end of this Trumpery, had not that last Service of Blackbirds, baked in good Pie-Crust with Raisins and Chessnuts, been brought up, and after them Quince-Peaches, so stuck with prickles, that they looked like Hedgehogs: Yet this might have been born with if the next Dish had not been such, that we had rather have starved than touched it: for when it was set upon the Table, and as we thought, a fat Goose, with Fishes and all kind of Fowl round it, 'whatever you see here,' said Trimalchio, 'is all made of the same substance'...

Quoth Trimalchio: 'Let me so grow in Estate not Bulk, as my Cook made all of this out of one Hog; there is not an excellenter fellow than himself; he shall, if he please, make ye a Poll of Ling of a Sow's Tripe; a Wood-Culver of fat Bacon; a Turtle of a Spring of Pork; and a Hen of a Collar of Brawn.'

PETRONIUS, *The Satyricon* (trans: by Burnaby).

JORROCKS IN FRANCE

AT LENGTH the diligence got its slow length dragged not only to Abbéville, but to the sign of the 'Fidèle Berger'—or 'Fiddle Burger,' as Mr. Jorrocks pronounced it—where they were to dine ...

The diligence being a *leetle* behind time as usual, the soup was on the table when they entered. The passengers quickly ranged themselves round, and, with his mouth watering as the female *garçon* lifted the cover from the tureen, Mr. Jorrocks sat in the expectation of seeing the rich contents ladled into the plates. His countenance fell fifty per cent. as the first spoonful passed before his eyes. 'My vig, why it's water!' exclaimed he—'water I do declare, with worms in it—I can't eat such stuff as that—it's not man's meat—oh! dear, oh! dear, I fear I've made a terrible mistake in coming to France! Never saw such stuff as this at Bleaden's or Birch's, or anywhere in the city.' 'I've travelled three hundred miles,' said the fat man, sending his plate from him in disgust, 'and never tasted such a mess as this before.' 'I'll show them up in *Bell's Life*,' cried Mr. Jorrocks; 'and look what stuff is here—beef boiled to rags! Well, I never, no never, saw anything like this before. Oh! I wish I was in Great Coram Street again.'—'I'm sure I can't live here—I wonder if I could get a return chaise—waiter—gar*soo*n —cuss! ...

Oh! Heavens! grant your poor Jorrocks but one request, and that is the contents of a single sentence. 'I want a roasted or boiled leg of mutton, beef, hung beef, a quarter of mutton, mutton chops, veal cutlets, stuffed tongue, hog's pudding, white sausage, chicken with rice, a nice fat roast fowl, roast chicken with cressy, roast or boiled pigeon, a fricassee of chicken, sweetbread, goose, lamb, calf's cheek, calf's head, fresh pork, salt pork, cold meat, hash.—But where's the use of titivating one's appetite with reading of such luxteries? . . . Oh! dear, oh! dear, I shall die of hunger I see—I shall die of absolute famine, my stomach thinks my throat's cut already!' In the height of his distress in came two turkeys and a couple of fowls, and his countenance shone forth like an April sun after a shower. 'Come, this is better,' said he; I'll trouble you, sir, for a leg and a wing, and a bit of the breast, for I'm really famished—oh, hang! the fellow's a Frenchman and I shall spend half the day in looking it out in my dictionary. Oh, dear, oh, dear, where's the dinner dialogue!—well, here's something to the purpose. 'I will send you a bit of this fowl.' 'A little bit of the fowl cannot hurt you.'—'No, nor a great bit either.'—'Which do you like best, a leg or a wing?' 'Qu'aimez vous le mieux, la cuisse ou l'aile?' Here the Countess Benvolio, who had been playing a good knife and fork herself, pricked up her ears, and, guessing at Jorrocks's wants, interceded with her countryman and got him a plateful of fowl. It was soon disposed of, however, and half a dish of hashed hare or cat, that was placed within reach of him shortly after, was quickly transferred into his plate . . .

Presently there was a large dish of stewed eels put on. 'What's that?' asked Jorrocks of the man. 'Poisson' was the reply. '*Poison!* why, you infidel, have you no conscience?' 'Fishe,' said the Countess. 'Oh aye, I smell—eels—just like what we have at the eel-pie house at Twickenham—your ladyship, I am thirsty—ge soif, in fact.' 'Ah, bon,' said the Countess laughing, and giving him a tumblerful of claret. 'I've travelled three hundred thousand miles,' said the fat man, 'and never saw claret drunk in that way before.' 'It's not werry good, I think,' said Mr. Jorrocks, smacking his lips; 'if it was not claret I would sooner drink port.' Some wild ducks and *fricandeau de veau* which followed were cut up and handed round, Jorrocks helping himself plentifully to both, as also to *pommes de terre à la maître d'hotel*, and bread at discretion... Just when Jorrocks began to think he had satisfied nature, in came a roast leg of mutton, a beef-steak, 'à la G——d dam,' and a dish of larks and snipes... He again set to, and 'went a good one' at both mutton and snipes, but on pulling up, he appeared somewhat exhausted... He had not got through it all yet however. Just as he was taking breath, a *garçon* entered with some custards and an enormous *omelette soufflée*, whose puffy brown sides bagged over the tin dish that contained it. 'There's a tart!' cried Mr. Jorrocks. 'Oh my eyes, what a swell! Well I suppose I must have a shy at it.——"In for a penny, in for a pound!" as we say at the Lord Mayor's feed. Know I shall be sick, but, however, here goes'... The first dive of the spoon undeceived him as he heard it sound at the bottom of the dish. 'Oh, lauk, what a go! All puff, by Jove!——a regular humbug——a balloon pudding in short! I won't eat such stuff——give it to Mouncheer there,' rejecting the offer of a piece. 'I like the solids;——will trouble you for some of that cheese, sir, and don't let it taste of the knife. But what do they mean by setting the dessert on before the cloth is removed?'...

'You shall take some dessert,' said the Countess,

handing him over some peaches and biscuits. 'Well, I'll try my hand at it if it will oblige your ladyship, but I really have had *almost* enough.' 'And some abricot,' said she, helping him to a couple of fine juicy ones. 'Oh, thank you, my lady, thank you, my lady, I'm *nearly* satisfied.' 'Vous ne mangez pas,' said she, giving him half a plate of grapes. 'Oh, my lady, you don't understand me—I *can't* eat any more—I am regularly high and dry—chock full—*bursting in fact.*' Here she handed him a plate of sponge cakes mixed with bon-bons and macaroons, saying 'Vous êtes un pauvre mangeur—vous ne mangez *rien*, Monsieur.' 'Oh, dear, she does not understand me, I see.—Indeed, my lady, I *can not* eat any more.—Ge would-era, se ge could-era, mais ge can-era pas!' 'Well now, I've travelled three hundred thousand miles, and never heard such a bit of French as that before,' said the fat man, chuckling.

SURTEES, *Jorrocks's Jaunts.*

A ROMAN BANQUET

THE DOCTOR ... with an air of infinite satisfaction, ... began:—'This here, gentlemen, is a boiled goose, served up in a sauce composed of pepper, lovage, coriander, mint, rue, anchovies, and oil! I wish for your sakes, gentlemen, it was one of the geese of Ferrara, so much celebrated among the ancients for the magnitude of their livers, one of which is said to have weighed upwards of two pounds; with this food, exquisite as it was, did the tyrant Heliogabalus regale his hounds. But I beg pardon. I had almost forgot the soup, which I hear is so necessary an article at all tables in France. At each end there are dishes of the falacacabia of the Romans; one is made of parsley, penny-royal, cheese, pine-tops, honey, vinegar, brine, eggs, cucumbers, onions, and hen-livers; the other is much the same as the *soup-maigre* of this country. Then there is a loin of veal boiled with fennel and caraway seed, on a pottage composed of pickle, oil, honey, and flour, and a curious *hachis* of the lights, liver and blood of an hare, together with a dish of roasted pigeons. Monsieur le Baron shall I help you to a plate of this soup?' The German, who did not all approve of the ingredients, assented to the proposal, and seemed to relish the composition; while the marquis ... was in consequence of his desire accommodated with a portion of the *soup-maigre*; and the count ... supplied himself with a pigeon ...

The Frenchman, having swallowed the first spoonful, made a pause; his throat swelled as if an egg had stuck in his gullet, his eyes rolled, and his mouth underwent a series of involuntary contractions and dilations. Pallet, who looked steadfastly at this connoisseur, with a view of consulting his taste, before he himself would venture upon the soup, began to be disturbed at these emotions, and observed with some concern, that the poor gentleman seemed to be going into a fit; when Peregrine assured him that these were symptoms of extasy, and for further confirmation, asked the marquis how he found the soup. It was with infinite difficulty that his complaisance could so far master his disgust, as to enable him to answer, 'Altogether excellent, upon my honour!' And the painter, being certified of his approbation, lifted the spoon to his mouth without scruple; but far from justifying the eulogium of his taster, when this precious composition diffused itself upon his palate, he seemed to be deprived of all sense and motion, and sat like the leaden statue of some river god, with the liquor flowing out at both sides of his mouth.

The doctor, alarmed at this indecent phenomenon, earnestly inquired into the cause of it; and when Pallet recovered his recollection, and swore that he would rather swallow porridge made of burning brimstone, than such an infernal mess as that which he had tasted; the physician, in his own vindication, assured the company, that, except the usual ingredients, he had mixed nothing in the soup but some sal-armoniac instead of the ancient nitrum, which could not now be procured; and appealed to the marquis, whether such a succedaneum was not an improvement of the whole. The unfortunate *petit-maître*, driven to the extremity of his condescension, acknowledged it to be a masterly refinement; and deeming himself obliged, in point of honour, to evince his sentiments by his practice, forced a few more mouthfuls of this disagreeable potion down his throat;

till his stomach was so much offended that he was compelled to start up of a sudden; and, in the hurry of his elevation, overturned his plate into the bosom of the baron. The emergency of his occasions would not permit him to stay and make apologies for this abrupt behaviour; so that he flew into another apartment, where Pickle found him puking, and crossing himself with great devotion; and a chair, at his desire, being brought to the door, he slipped into it, more dead than alive ... When our hero returned to the dining-room ... the places were filled with two pies, one of dormice liquored with syrup of white poppies which the doctor had substituted in the room of toasted poppy-seed, formerly eaten with honey, as a dessert; and the other composed of a hock of pork baked in honey.

Pallet hearing the first of these dishes described, lifting up his hands and eyes, and with signs of loathing and amazement pronounced, 'A pye made of dormice and syrup of poppies; Lord in heaven! what beastly fellows those Romans were!' ... All the doctor's invitations and assurances could not prevail upon his guests to honour the *hachis* and the goose; and that course was succeeded by another... 'That which smoaks in the middle,' said he, 'is a sow's stomach, filled with a composition of minced pork, hogs brains, eggs, pepper, cloves, garlick, aniseed, rue, oil, wine, and pickle. On the right-hand side are the teats and belly of a sow, just farrowed, fried with sweet wine, oil, flour, lovage, and pepper. On the left is a fricasee of snails, fed, or rather purged, with milk. At that end next Mr. Pallet are fritters of pompions, lovage, origanum, and oil; and here are a couple of pullets, roasted and stuffed in the manner of Apicius.'

The painter, who had by wry faces testified his abhorrence of the sow's stomach, which he compared to a bagpipe, and the snails which had undergone purgation, no sooner heard him mention the roasted pullets, than he eagerly solicited the wing of a fowl; . . . but scarce were they set down before him, when the tears ran down his cheeks, and he called aloud in a manifest disorder, 'Z——ds! this is the essence of a whole bed of garlic!' That he might not, however, disappoint or disgrace the entertainer, he applied his instruments to one of the birds; and when he opened up the cavity, was assaulted by such an irruption of intolerable smells, that, without staying to disengage himself from the cloth, he sprung away, with an exclamation of 'Lord Jesus!' and involved the whole table in havoc, ruin, and confusion.

Before Pickle could accomplish his escape, he was sauced with the syrup of the dormouse-pye, which went to pieces in the general wreck; and as for the Italian count, he was overwhelmed by the sow's stomach, which bursting in the fall, discharged its contents upon his leg and thigh, and scalded him so miserably, that he shrieked with anguish, and grinned with a most ghastly and horrible aspect. . .

The doctor was confounded with shame and vexation . . . he expressed his sorrow for the misadventure . . . and protested there was nothing in the fowls which could give offence to a sensible nose, the stuffing being a mixture of pepper, lovage, and assafœtida, and the sauce consisting of wine and herring-pickle, which he had used instead of the celebrated garum of the Romans.

SMOLLETT, *Peregrine Pickle*.

A CHRISTMAS DINNER

SUCH A BUSTLE ensued you might have thought a goose the rarest of all birds; a feathered phenomenon, to which a black swan was a matter of course—and in truth it was something very like it in that house. Mrs. Crachit made the gravy (ready beforehand in a little saucepan) hissing hot; Master Peter mashed the potatoes with incredible vigour; Miss Belinda sweetened up the apple-sauce; Martha dusted the hot plates; Bob took Tiny Tim beside him in a tiny corner at the table; the two young Crachits set chairs for everybody, not forgetting themselves, and mounting guard upon their posts, crammed spoons into their mouths, lest they should shriek for goose before their turn came to be helped. At last the dishes were set on, and grace was said. It was succeeded by a breathless pause, as Mrs. Crachit, looking slowly all along the carving knife, prepared to plunge it into the breast; but when she did, and when the long expected gush of stuffing issued forth, one murmur of delight arose all round the board, and even Tiny Tim, excited by the two young Crachits, beat on the table with the handle of his knife, and feebly cried Hurrah!

There was never such a goose. Bob said he didn't believe there was ever such a goose cooked. Its tenderness and flavour, size and cheapness, were the themes of universal admiration. Eked out by apple sauce and mashed potatoes, it was a sufficient dinner for the whole family: indeed as Mrs. Crachit said with great delight (surveying one small atom of a bone upon the dish) they hadn't ate it all at last! Yet everyone had had enough, and the youngest Crachits in particular, were steeped in sage and onion to the eyebrows! But now, the plates being changed by Miss Belinda, Mrs. Crachit left the room alone—too nervous to bear witnesses—to take the pudding up and bring it in.

Suppose it should not be done enough! Suppose it should break in turning out! Suppose somebody should have got over the wall of the backyard and stolen it, while they were merry with the goose—a supposition at which the two young Crachits became livid! All sorts of horrors were supposed.

Hallo! A great deal of steam! The pudding was out of the copper. A smell like washing day! That was the cloth. A smell like an eating-house and a pastrycook's next door to each other, with a laundress's next door to that! That was the pudding! In half a minute Mrs. Crachit entered—flushed, but smiling proudly—with the pudding, like a speckled cannon-ball, so hard and firm, blazing in half of half-a-quartern of ignited brandy, and bedight with Christmas holly stuck into the top.

Oh, a wonderful pudding! Bob Crachit said, and calmly too, that he regarded it as the greatest success achieved by Mrs. Crachit since their marriage. Mrs. Crachit said that now the weight was off her mind, she would confess that she had had her doubts about the quantity of flour. Everybody had something to say about it, but nobody said or thought it was at all a small pudding for a large family. It would have been flat heresy to do so. Any Crachit would have blushed to hint at such a thing.

DICKENS, *A Christmas Carol.*

DOCTOR FOLLIOTT AT DINNER

THE REV. DR. FOLLIOTT: Here is a very fine salmon before me: and May is the very *point nommé* to have salmon in perfection. There is a fine turbot close by, and there is much to be said in his behalf; but salmon in May is the king of fish.

Mr. Crotchet: That salmon before you, doctor, was caught in the Thames this morning.

The Rev. Dr. Folliott: Rarity of rarities! A Thames salmon caught this morning. Now, Mr. MacQuedy, even in fish your Modern Athens must yield. *Cedite Graii.*

Mr. MacQuedy: Eh! sir, on its own ground, your Thames salmon has two virtues over all others: first, that it is fresh; and, second, that it is rare; for I understand you do not take half-a-dozen in a year.

The Rev. Dr. Folliott: In some years, sir, not one. Mud, filth, gas dregs, lock-weirs, and the march of mind, developed in the form of poaching, have ruined the fishery. But when we do catch a salmon, happy the man to whom he falls.

Mr. MacQuedy: I confess, sir, this is excellent; but I cannot see why it should be better than a Tweed salmon at Kelso.

The Rev. Dr. Folliott: Sir, I will take a glass of Hock with you.

Mr. MacQuedy: With all my heart, sir. There are several varieties of the salmon genus: but the common salmon, the *salmo salar*, is only one species, one and the same everywhere, just like the human mind. Locality and education make all the difference...

Mr. Crotchet, Jun.: Champagne, doctor?

The Rev. Dr. Folliott: Most willingly. But you will permit my drinking it while it sparkles. I hold it a heresy to let it deaden in my hand, while the glass of my *compotator* is being filled on the opposite side of the table. By-the-bye, captain, you remember a passage in Athenæus, where he cites Menander on the subject of fish-sauce: (*The captain was aghast for an answer that would satisfy both his neighbours, when he was relieved by the divine continuing.*) The science of fish sauce, Mr. MacQuedy, is by no means brought to perfection; a fine field of discovery still lies open in that line.

Mr. MacQuedy: Nay, sir, beyond lobster sauce, I take it ye cannot go.

The Rev. Dr. Folliott: In their line, I grant you, oyster and lobster sauce are the pillars of Hercules. But I speak of the cruet sauces, where the quintessence of the sapid is condensed in a phial. I can taste in my mind's palate a combination, which, if I could give it reality, I would christen with the name of my college, and hand it down to posterity as a seat of learning indeed.

PEACOCK, *Crochet Castle.*

THOMAS WALKER'S WHITEBAIT DINNER

I WILL GIVE YOU, dear reader, an account of a dinner I have ordered this very day at Lovegrove's at Blackwall... The party will consist of seven men beside myself, and every guest is asked for some reason —upon which good fellowship mainly depends, for people brought together unconnectedly had, in my opinion, better be kept separate...

The dinner is to consist of turtle followed by no other fish but whitebait, which is to be followed by no other meat but grouse, which are to be succeeded simply by apple fritters and jelly, pastry on such occasions being quite out of place. With the turtle of course there will be punch, with the whitebait, champagne, and with the grouse, claret... I shall permit no other wines, unless perchance a bottle of port... With respect to the adjuncts, I shall take care that there is cayenne, with lemon cut in halves, not in quarters, within reach of everyone, for the turtle, and that brown bread and butter in abundance is set upon the table for the whitebait. It is no trouble to think of these little matters beforehand, but they make a vast difference in convivial contentment. The dinner will be followed by ices and a good dessert, and after which, coffee and one glass of liqueur each and no more; so that the present may be enjoyed rationally without introducing retrospective regrets. If the master of a feast wishes his party to succeed he must know how to command, and not let his guests run riot each according to his own wild fancy. Such, reader, is my idea of a dinner, of which I hope you approve.

WALKER, *The Original*.

LUNCH AT COMBRAY

FROM THE DAY on which fine weather definitely set in at Combray—the proud hour of noon, descending from the steeple of Saint-Hilaire which it blazoned for a moment with the twelve points of its sonorous crown, would long have echoed about our table ... and we would still be found seated in front of our Arabian Nights plates, weighted down by the heat of the day, and even more by our heavy meal. For the permanent foundation of eggs, cutlets, potatoes, preserves and biscuits, whose appearance on the table she no longer announced to us, Françoise would add—as the labour of fields and orchards, the harvest of the tides, the luck of the market, the kindness of the neighbours, and her own genius might provide; and so effectively that our bill of fare, like the quatrefoils that were carved on the porches of cathedrals in the thirteenth century, reflected to some extent the march of the seasons and the incidents of human life—a brill, because the fish-woman had guaranteed its freshness; a turkey, because she had seen a beauty in the market; ... cardoons with marrow, because she had never done them for us that way before; a roast leg of mutton, because the fresh air made one hungry and there would be plenty of time for it to 'settle down' in the seven hours before dinner; spinach, by way of a change; apricots, because they were still hard to get; gooseberries, because in another fortnight there would be none left; raspberries, which Mr. Swann had brought specially; cherries, the first to come from the cherry tree which had yielded none for the last two years; a cream-cheese, of which in those days I was extremely fond; an almond cake, because she had ordered one the evening before; a fancy loaf, because it was our turn to 'offer' the holy bread. And when all these had been eaten, a work composed expressly for ourselves, but dedicated more particularly to my father who had a fondness for such things—a cream of chocolate, inspired in the mind, created by the hand of Françoise, would be laid before us, light and fleeting as an occasional piece of music, into which she had poured the whole of her talent. Anyone who refused to partake of it, saying: 'No, thank you, I have finished, I am not hungry,' would at once have been lowered to the level of the Philistines who, when an artist makes them a present of one of his works, examine its weight and material, whereas what is of value is the creator's intention and his signature. To have left even the tiniest morsel in the dish would have shewn as much discourtesy as to rise and leave a concert hall while the piece was still being played, and under the composer's very eyes.

PROUST, *Swann's Way* (trans: by Scott Moncrieff).

EASTER SUNDAY WITH JOHNSON

TO MY GREAT SURPRISE he asked me to dine with him on Easter Day. I never supposed that he had a dinner at his house; for I had not then heard of any one of his friends having been entertained at his table. He told me, 'I generally have a meat pie on Sunday: it is baked at a public oven, which is very properly allowed, because one man can attend it; and thus the advantage is obtained of not keeping servants from Church to dress dinners.

April 11, being Easter Sunday, after having attended divine service at St. Paul's, I repaired to Dr. Johnson's. I had gratified my curiosity much in dining with Jean Jaques Rousseau, while he lived in the wilds of Neufchâtel: I had as great a curiosity to dine with Dr. Samuel Johnson, in the dusky recess of a court in Fleet Street. I supposed we should scarcely have knives and forks, and only some strange, uncouth, ill-drest dish: but I found everything in very good order. We had no other company but Mrs. Williams and a young woman whom I did not know. As a dinner here was considered as a singular phenomenon, and as I was frequently interrogated on the subject, my readers may perhaps be desirous to know our bill of fare. Foote, I remember, in allusion to Francis, the *negro*, was willing to suppose that our repast was *black broth*. But the fact was, that we had a very good soup, a boiled leg of lamb and spinach, a veal pie, and a rice pudding.

BOSWELL, *Life of Samuel Johnson.*

A FEAST IN PARADISE

AND EVE within, due at her hour prepar'd
   For dinner savourie fruits, of taste to please
   True appetite, and not disrelish thirst
Of nectarous draughts between, from milkie stream,
Berrie or Grape: to whom thus Adam call'd.

  Haste hither Eve, and worth thy sight behold
Eastward among those Trees, what glorious shape
Comes this way moving; seems another Morn
Ris'n on mid-noon; som great behest from Heav'n
To us perhaps he brings, and will voutsafe
This day to be our Guest. But goe with speed,
And what thy stores contain, bring forth and poure
Abundance, fit to honour and receive
Our Heav'nly stranger ...

  To whom thus Eve. Adam, earths hallowd mould,
Of God inspir'd, small store will serve, where store,
All seasons, ripe for use hangs on the stalk;
Save what by frugal storing firmness gains
To nourish, and superfluous moist consumes:
But I will haste and from each bough and break,
Each Plant and juciest Gourd will pluck such choice
To entertain our Angel guest, as hee
Beholding shall confess that here on Earth
God hath dispenst his bounties as in Heav'n.

  So saying, with dispatchful looks in haste
She turns, on hospitable thoughts intent
What choice to chuse for delicacie best,
What order, so contriv'd as not to mix
Tastes, not well joynd, inelegant, but bring
Taste after taste upheld with kindliest change,

Bestirs her then, and from each tender stalk
Whatever Earth all-bearing Mother yeilds
In India East or West, or middle shoare
In Pontus or the Punic Coast, or where
Alcinous reign'd, fruit of all kindes, in coate,
Rough, or smooth rin'd, or bearded husk, or shell
She gathers, Tribute large, and on the board
Heaps with unsparing hand; for drink the Grape
She crushes, inoffensive moust, and meathes
From many a berrie, and from sweet kernels prest
She tempers dulcet creams, nor these to hold
Wants her fit vessels pure, then, strews the ground
With Rose and Odours from the shrub unfum'd . . .

          So to the Silvan Lodge
They came, that like Pomona's Arbour smil'd
With flourets deck'd and fragrant smells; but Eve
Undeckt, save with herself, more lovely fair
Then Wood-Nymph, or the fairest Goddess feign'd
Of three that in Mount Ida naked strove . . .

          Rais'd of grassie terf
Thir Table was, and mossie seats had round,
And on her ample Square from side to side
All Autumn pil'd, though Spring and Autumn here
Danc'd hand in hand.

      MILTON, *Paradise Lost.*

II: REPAS GALANTS

Cupid and Bacchus my Saints are;
May Drink and Love still reign.
With Wine I wash away my Cares
And then to Love again...

                                    ROCHESTER.

A WHITE DINNER

'I DECLARED myself to her,' said Alcide, laying his hand on his heart, 'in a manner which was as novel as I am charmed to think it was agreeable. Where cannot Love penetrate, respectable Madame Frisbi? Cupid is the father of the invention! I inquired of the domestics what were the *plats* of which Mademoiselle partook with most pleasure; and built up my little battery accordingly. On a day when her parents had gone to dine in the world (and I am grieved to say that a grosser dinner in a restaurant, on the Boulevard, or in the Palais-Royal, seemed to form the delights of these unrefined persons), the charming Miss entertained some comrades of the pension; and I advised myself to send up a little repast suitable to so delicate young palates. Her lovely name is Blanche. The veil of the maiden is white, the wreath of roses she wears is white. I determined that my dinner should be as spotless as the snow. At her accustomed hour, and instead of the rude *gigot à l'eau* which was ordinarily served at her too simple table, I sent her up a little *potage à la reine blanche* I called it—as white as her own tint—and confectioned with the most fragrant cream and almonds. I then offered up at her shrine a *filet de merlan à l'agnés*, and a delicate *plat*, which I have designated as *Eperlan à la Sainte Thérèse*, and of which my charming Miss partook with pleasure. I followed this by two little *entrées* of sweetbread and chicken; and the only brown thing which I permitted myself in the entertainment was a little roast of lamb, which I laid in a meadow of spinaches, surrounded with *croustillons*, representing sheep, and ornamented with daisies and other savage flowers. After this came my second service: a pudding *à la Reine Elisabeth* (who, Madame Frisbi knows, was a maiden princess); a dish of opal-coloured plover's eggs, which I called *Nid de tourtereaux à la Roucoule;* placing in the midst of them two of those tender volatiles, billing each other, and confectioned with butter; a basket containing little *gâteaux* of apricots, which, I know, all young ladies adore; and a jelly of marasquin, bland, insinuating, intoxicating as the glance of beauty. This I designated *Ambroisie de Calypso à la Souveraine de mon Cœur*. And when the ice was brought in—an ice of *plombière* and cherries—how do you think I had shaped them, Madame Frisbi? In the form of two hearts united with an arrow, on which I had laid, before it entered, a bridal veil in cut paper, surmounted by a wreath of virginal orange-flowers. I stood at the door to watch the effect of this entry. It was but one cry of admiration. The three young ladies filled their glasses with the sparkling Ay, and carried me in a toast. I heard it, I heard Miss speak of me—I heard her say, "Tell Monsieur Mirobolant that we thank him—we admire him—we love him!" My feet almost failed me as she spoke.'

THACKERAY, *Pendennis*.

TOM JONES CAPTIVATED

WE THINK it no disparagement to our hero to mention the immoderate ardour with which he laid about him at this season: indeed, it may be doubted whether Ulysses, who, by the way, seems to have had the best stomach of all the heroes in that eating poem of the Odyssey, ever made a better meal. Three pounds, at least, of flesh which formerly had contributed to the composition of an ox, was how honoured with becoming part of the individual Mr. Jones...

Mrs. Waters had, in truth, not only a good opinion of our hero, but a very great affection for him; to speak out boldly at once, she was in love, according to the present universally received sense of that phrase, by which love is applied indiscriminately to the desirable objects of all our passions, appetites, and senses, and is understood to be that preference which we give to one kind of food rather than to another. But though the love to these several objects may possibly be one and the same in all cases, its operation must be allowed to be different; for, how much so ever we may be in love with an excellent sirloin of beef, or bottle of Burgundy; with a damask rose, or Cremona fiddle; yet do we never smile, nor ogle, nor dress, nor flatter, nor endeavour by any other arts or tricks to gain the affection of the said beef, etc... Say then, ye Graces?... say what were the weapons used to captivate the heart of Mr. Jones. First, from two lovely blue eyes, whose bright orbs flashed lightning at their discharge flew forth two pointed ogles; but, happily for our hero, hit only a vast piece of beef which he was then conveying into his plate, and harmless spent their force. The fair warrior perceived their miscarriage and immediately from her fair bosom drew forth a deadly sigh; a sigh which none could have heard unmoved, and which was sufficient at once to have swept off a dozen *beaux*; so soft, so sweet, so tender, that the insinuating air must have its subtle way to the heart of our hero, had it not luckily have been driven from his ears by the coarse bubbling of some bottled ale, which at that time he was pouring forth. Many other weapons did she essay; but the god of eating, if there be such deity, for I do not confidently assert it, preserved his votary; or perhaps, it may not be *dignus vindice nodus*, and the present security of Jones may be accounted for by natural means; for as love frequently preserves from the attacks of hunger, so may hunger possibly, in some cases, defend us against love.

The fair one, enraged at her frequent disappointments, determined on a short cessation of arms; which interval she employed in making ready every engine of amorous warfare for the renewing of the attack, when dinner should be over. No sooner, then, was the cloth removed, than she again began her operations. First, having planted her right eye sideways against Mr. Jones, she shot from its corner a most penetrating glance; which, though great part of its force was spent before it reached our hero, did not vent itself absolutely without effect. This the fair one perceiving, hastily withdrew her eyes, and levelled them downwards, as if she was concerned for what she had done; though by this means she designed only to draw him from his guard, and, indeed, to open his eyes, through which she intended to surprise his heart. And now, gently lifting up those two bright orbs, which had already begun to make an impression on poor Jones, she discharged a volley of small charms at once from her whole countenance in a smile; not a smile of mirth, nor of joy, but a smile of affection, which most ladies have always ready at their command, and which serves them to show at once their good humour, their pretty dimples, and their white teeth. This smile our hero received full in his eyes, and was immediately staggered with its force. He then began to see the designs of the enemy, and, indeed, to feel their success. A parley was now set on foot between the parties; during which, the artful fair so slyly and imperceptibly carried on her attack, that she had almost subdued the heart of our hero before she again repaired to acts of hostility. To confess the truth, I am afraid Mr. Jones maintained a kind of Dutch defence, and treacherously delivered up the garrison, without duly weighing his allegiance to the fair Sophia. In short, no sooner had the amorous parley ended, and the lady had unmasked the royal battery, by carelessly letting her handkerchief drop from her neck, than the heart of Mr. Jones was entirely taken, and the fair conqueror enjoyed the usual fruits of her victory.

FIELDING, *Tom Jones*.

A RENDEZVOUS IN A BATH

WHEN THE HOURE for their meeting was come, he went unto the place where he was appointed, a Bathe (belike) best agreeing with such businesse.

Not long had he taried there, but two Women slaves came laden to him, the one bearing a Mattresse of fine Fustian on hir head, and the other a great Basket filled with many things. Having spred the Mattresse in a faire Chamber on a Couch-bed, they covered it with delicate white linnen sheets, all about embroidred with faire Fringes of gold, then laid they on costly quilts of rich Silkes, artificially wrought with gold and silver knots, having pearles and precious stones interwoven among them, and two such rich pillowes, as sildome before had the like bin seene. Salabetto putting off his garments, entred the Bathe prepared for him, where the two Slaves washed his body very neatly. Soone after came Biancafiore hirselfe, attended on by two other women slaves, and seeing Salabetto in the Bathe, making him a lowly reverence, breathing forth infinite dissembled sighes, and teares trickling down her cheekes, kissing and embracing him, thus she spake.

I know not what man else in the worlde, beside thy selfe, could have the power to bring me hither; the fire flew from thy faire eies (O thou incomparable lovely Tuscane) that melted my soule, and makes me onely live at thy command. Then hurling off her light wearing garment (because she came prepared for the purpose) she stept into the bathe to him, and not permitting the slaves a-while to come neere, none but herselfe must now lave his body, with Muske compounded sope and Gillyfloures. Afterwards the slaves washed both him and her, bringing two goodly sheetes softe and white, yeelding such a delicate smell of Roses, even as if they had bene made of Rose-leaves. In the one they folded Salabetto, and her in the other, and so conveyed them on their shoulders unto the prepared Bed-Couch, where because they should not sweate any longer, they tooke the sheetes from about them, and laid them gently in the bed.

Then they opened the Basket, wherein were divers goodly Silver bottles, some filled with Rosewaters, others with flowers of Oranges, and waters distilled of Gelsomine, Muske, and Amber-Greece, wherewith (againe) the slaves bathed their bodyes in the bed, and afterwards presented them with a variety of Comfites, as also very precious Wines, serving them in stead of a little Collation. Salabetto supposed himself to be in Paradise: for this appeared to be no earthly joy, bestowing a thousand gladsome gazes on her, who (questionlesse) was a most beautiful creature, and the tarrying of the Slaves, seemed a million of yeares to him, that he might more freely embrace his Biancafiore...

When she thought it convenient time to depart thence, the slaves returned; they cloathed themselves, and had a Banquet standing ready prepared for them, where-with they cheared their wearyed spirits, after they had first washed in odorifferous waters. At parting, Salabetto (quoth she) whensoever thy leysures shal best serve thee, I will repute it as my cheefest happinesse, that thou wilt accept a Supper and Lodging in my house, which let it be this instant night, if thou canst. He being absolutely caught both by her beauty and flattering behaviour,

beleeved faithfuly that he was as entirely beloved of her,
as the heart is of the body: whereupon he thus answered.
Madame, whatsoever pleaseth you, must needes be
much more acceptable unto me: and therefore not
onely may command my service this night, but likewise
the whole employment of my life, to be onely yours in
my very best studies and endeavours.

No sooner did she heare this answer, but she returned
home to her owne house, which she decked in most
sumptuous manner, and also made ready a costly
Supper, expecting the arrivall of Salabetto: who when
the dark night was indifferently well entred, went
thither and was welcommed with wonderfull kindnesse,
wanting no costly Wines and delicates all the Supper
while.

BOCCACCIO, *The Decameron*

AN APHRODISIAC DIET

A RARE THING to see a young man or woman that lives idly and fares well, of what condition soever not to be in love. Alcibiades was still dallying with wanton young women, immoderate in his expenses, effeminate in his apparel, ever in love, but why? he was over-delicate in his diet, too frequent and excessive in banquets. Lust and security domineer together, as St. Hierome averreth. All which the Wife of Bath in Chaucer freely justifies:

> *For all to sicker, as cold engrendreth hail,*
> *A liquorish tongue must have a liquorish tail.*

Especially if they shall further it by choice diet, as many times those Sybarites and Phæaces do, feed liberally, and by their good will eat nothing but lascivious meats. (First and foremost, strong wine, vegetables, beans, roots of all kinds, well seasoned and with plenty of pepper, garden radishes, lettuces, rocket, rapes, leeks, onions, pine-nuts, sweet almonds, electuaries, syrups, juices, snails, shell-fish, fish tastefully cooked, poultry, testicles of animals, eggs, various sauces, soft beds and couches, etc. Also ... more delicate dishes, mulled wine, choice fruits, scents, cakes, essences more tasty than wine, and all the products of the kitchen, the chemist's shop, or any other factory.)

BURTON, *The Anatomy of Melancholy.*

A BANQUET

AT EVERY TIME we were assembled together ... you are not able to imagine what sumptuous hangings of tapestrie did adorn the Hall where we sate at meate, the Tables covered in such Royall manner, waited on by numberless noble and goodly attendants, both women and men, serving readily, at each man's command of the company. The Basins, Ewers, Pots, Flagons, and all the vessels else which stood before, and for the service of our diet being composed onely of Gold and Silver, and out of no worse did we both eate and drink: the viands being very rare and dainty, abounding in plenty and variety, according to the appetite of everie person, as nothing could be wished for but it was instantly obtained.

In good sadness, Sir, I am not able to remember and tell you (within the compass of a thousand years) what and how manie severall kindes of Musicall Instruments were continually played on before us: what multiplicity of wax lights burned in all partes of the roomes; neither the excessive store of rich Drugs, Marchpanes, Comfites, and rare Banquetting stuffe, consumed there at one Feasting, wherein there wanted no bounty of the best and purest wines...

Not any one man among us, but appeared by his apparell equall to the greatest Emperor on the earth, his robe most sumptuously embroidered with precious stones, Pearles, and Carbuncles, as the world affordeth not the like. But above all the rest, the delights and pleasures there are beyond my capacity to expresse, or (indeede) any comparison: as namely, store of goodly and beautifull women, brought hither from all parts of the world: always provided if men bee desirous of their company...

Now I am further to tell you, that after we have tasted a Cup of precious Wine, fed on a few delicate Comfits, and danced a dance or two to the rare Musicke: everyone taketh a Lady by the hand, of whom he pleaseth to make his election, and she conducteth him to her Chamber, in very grave and gracious manner. Concerning the Chambers there, each of them resembleth a Paradise to looke on, they are so faire and goodly, and no lesse odiferous in smell, then the sweetest perfumes in your Apothecaries shoppes, or the rare compounds of Spices, when they are beaten in an open morter. And as for the Beds, they are infinitely richer, than the very costliest belonging to the Duke of Venice: yet (in such) each man is appointed to take his rest, the Musicke of rare Cymbals lasting all night long, much better to be by you considered, then in my rude eloquence expressed.

BOCCACCIO, *The Decameron*

THE PREPARATION OF VENUS

WHEN I was within the house I found my dear and sweet Fotis mincing of meat and making pottage for her master and mistresse, the Cupboard was all set with wines, and I thought I smelled the savour of some dainty meats: she had about her middle a white and clean apron, and shee was girded about her body under the paps with a swathell of red silke, and she stirred the pot and turned the meat with her faire and white hands, in such sort that with stirring and turning the same, her loynes and hips did likewise move and shake, which was in my mind a comely sight to see . . . wherewithall I rose up and went into my chamber, where I found all things finely prepared. . . The table was all covered with those meats that were left at supper, the cups were filled halfe full with water, to temper and delay the wines, the flaggon stood ready prepared, and there lacked nothing that was necessary for the preparation of Venus. And when I was entring the bed, behold my Fotis (who had brought her mistresse to bed) came in and gave me roses and floures which she had in her apron, and some she threw about the bed, and kissed mee sweetly, and tied a garland about my head, and bespred the chamber with the residue. Which when shee had done, shee took a cup of wine and delaied it with hot water, and profered it me to drinke; and before I had drunk off all she pulled it from my mouth, and then gave it me againe, and in this manner we emptied the pot twice or thrice together.

APULEIUS, *The Golden Asse* (trans: by Adlington).

BECKY SETS HER CAP AT A RICH ANGLO-INDIAN

DOWNSTAIRS, then they went, Joseph very red and blushing, Rebecca very modest, and holding her green eyes downwards. She was dressed in white with bare shoulders as white as snow—the picture of youth, unprotected innocence, & humble, virgin simplicity. 'I must be very quiet,' thought Rebecca, 'and very much interested about India.'

Now we have heard how Mrs. Sedley had prepared a fine curry for her son, just as he liked it, and in the course of dinner a portion of this dish was offered to Rebecca. 'What is it?' said she, turning an appealing look to Mr. Joseph.

'Capital,' said he. His mouth was full of it; his face quite red with the delightful exercise of gobbling. 'Mother, it's as good as my own curries in India.'

'Oh, I must try some, if it is an Indian dish,' said Miss Rebecca. 'I am sure everything must be good that comes from there.'

'Give Miss Sharp some curry, my dear,' said Mr. Sedley laughing.

Rebecca had never tasted the dish before.

'Do you find it as good as everything else from India?' said Mr. Sedley.

'Oh, excellent,' said Rebecca, who was suffering tortures with the cayenne pepper.

'Try a chili with it, Miss Sharp,' said Joseph, really interested.

'A chili!' said Rebecca gasping, 'Oh, yes!' She thought a chili was something cool, as its name imported, and was served with some. 'How fresh and green they look,' she said, and put one into her mouth. It was hotter than the curry; flesh and blood could bear it no longer. She laid down her fork. 'Water, for Heaven's sake, water!' she cried. Mr. Sedley burst out laughing (he was a coarse man from the Stock Exchange, where they love all sorts of practical jokes). 'They are real Indian, I assure you,' said he. 'Sambo, give Miss Sharp some water.'

The paternal laugh was echoed by Joseph, who thought the joke capital. The ladies only smiled a little, they thought poor Rebecca suffered too much. She would have liked to choke old Sedley, but she swallowed her mortification as well as she had the abominable curry before it, and as soon as she could speak said with a comical, good-humoured air—

'I ought to have remembered the pepper which the Princess of Persia puts in the cream-tarts in the Arabian Nights. Do you put cayenne into your cream-tarts in India, Sir?'

Old Sedley began to laugh, and thought Rebecca was a good-humoured girl. Joseph simply said, 'Cream tarts, Miss? Our cream is very bad in Bengal. We generally use goat's milk, and gad! do you know, I've got to prefer it!'

'You won't like *everything* from India now, Miss Sharp,' said the old gentleman; but when the ladies had retired after dinner, the wily old fellow said to his son, 'Have a care, Joe, that girl is setting her cap at you.'

THACKERAY, *Vanity Fair*.

ULYSSES ENTERTAINED BY CIRCE

THEN Mercury went back to high Olympus passing over the wooded island; but I fared onward to the house of Circe, and my heart was clouded with care as I walked along. When I got to the gates I stood there and called the Goddess, and as soon as she heard me she came down, opened the door, and asked me to come in; so I followed her, much troubled in my mind. She set me on a richly decorated seat inlaid with silver, there was a footstool also under my feet, and she mixed a mess in a golden goblet for me to drink; but she drugged it, for she meant me mischief. When she had given it me and I had drunk it without its charming me, she struck me with her wand. 'There now,' she cried, 'be off to the pigstye, and make your lair with the rest of them.'

But I rushed at her with my sword drawn as though I would kill her, whereon she fell with a loud scream, clasped my knees, and spoke piteously, saying, 'Who and whence are you? from what place and people have you come? How can it be that my drugs have no power to charm you? Never yet was any man able to stand so much as a taste of the herb I gave you; you must be spellproof; surely you can be none other than the bold hero Ulysses, who Mercury always said would come here one day with his ship while on his way home from Troy; so be it then; sheathe your sword and let us go to bed, that we may make friends and learn to trust each other.'

And I answered, 'Circe, how can you expect me to be friendly with you when you have just been turning all my men into pigs? . . .

'I shall not consent to go to bed with you unless you will first take your solemn oath to plot no further harm against me.'

So she swore at once as I had told her, and when she had completed her oath then I went to bed with her.

Meanwhile her four servants, who are her housemaids, set about their work. They are the children of the groves and fountains and of the holy waters that run down into the sea. One of them spread a fair purple cloth over a seat, and laid a carpet underneath it. Another brought tables of silver up to the seats and set them with baskets of gold. A third mixed some sweet wine with water in a silver bowl and put golden cups upon the tables while the fourth brought in water and set it to boil in a large cauldron over a good fire which she had lighted. When the water in the cauldron was boiling she poured cold into it till it was just as I liked it, and then she set me in a bath and began washing me from the cauldron about the head and shoulders to take the tire and stiffness out of my limbs. As soon as she had done washing me and anointing me with oil, she arrayed me in a good cloak and shirt and led me to a richly decorated seat inlaid with silver; there was a footstool also under my feet. A maid servant then brought me water in a beautiful golden ewer and poured it into a silver basin for me to wash my hands, and she drew a clean table beside me; an upper servant brought me bread and offered me many good things of what there was in the house, and then Circe bade me eat.

HOMER, *The Odyssey* (trans: by Samuel Butler)

FROM THE SONG OF SONGS

How fair and how pleasant art thou, O love, for delights!

This thy stature is like to a palm tree, and thy breasts to clusters of grapes.

I said, I will go up to the palm tree, I will take hold of the boughs thereof: now also thy breasts shall be as clusters of the vine, and the smell of thy nose like apples;

And the roof of thy mouth like the best wine for my beloved, that goeth down sweetly, causing the lips of those that are asleep to speak.

I am my beloved's, and his desire is toward me.

Come, my beloved, let us go forth into the field; let us lodge in the villages.

Let us get up early to the vineyards; let us see if the vine flourish, whether the tender grape appear, and the pomegranates bud forth: there will I give thee my loves.

The mandrakes give a smell, and at our gates are all manner of pleasant fruits, new and old, which I have laid up for thee, O my beloved.

Holy Bible (Authorised Version).

FEAST OF ST. AGNES

A CASEMENT high and triple-arch'd there was,
All garlanded with carven imag'ries
Of fruit, and flowers, and bunches of knot-grass . . .

Full on this casement shone the wintry moon,
And threw warm gules on Madeline's fair breast
As down she knelt for heaven's grace and boon . . .

Soon, trembling in her soft and chilly nest,
In sort of wakeful swoon, perplex'd she lay,
Until the poppied warmth of sleep oppress'd
Her soothed limbs, and soul fatigued away . . .

Stol'n to this paradise, and so entranced,
Porphyro gazed upon her empty dress,
And listened to her breathing, if it chanced
To wake into a slumberous tenderness . . .

Then by the bedside, where the faded moon
Made a dim, silver, twilight, soft he set
A table, and half anguish'd threw thereon
A cloth of woven crimson, gold and jet . . .

And still she slept, an azure-lidded sleep,
In blanched linen, smooth and lavender'd,
While he from forth the closet brought a heap
Of candied apple, quince, and plum, and gourd:
With jellies soother than the creamy curd,
And lucent syrops, tinct with cinnamon;
Manna and dates, in argosy transferr'd
From Fez; and spiced dainties, every one,
From silken Samarkand to cedared Lebanon.

These delicates he heap'd with glowing hand
On golden dishes and in baskets bright
Of wreathed silver: sumptuous they stand
In the retired quiet of the night,
Filling the chilly room with perfume light.
'And now, my love, my seraph fair, awake!
Thou art my heaven, and I thy eremite;
Open thine eyes, for meek St. Agnes' sake.'

    KEATS, *The Eve of St. Agnes*.

LA POULARDE DE BRESSE

DEUX JEUNES ÉPOUX avaient assisté à un grand déjeuner d'huîtres; ... on sait ce que cela veut dire. Ces repas sont charmants ... mais ils ont l'inconvénient de déranger toutes les opérations de la journée. C'est ce qui arriva dans cette occasion. L'heure du diner étant venue, les époux se mirent à table; mais ce ne fut que pour la forme. Madame mangea un peu de potage, Monsieur but un verre de vin rougie; quelques amis survinrent, on fit une partie de whist, la soirée se passa, et le même lit reçut les deux époux.

Vers deux heures du matin Monsieur se réveilla; il était mal à son aise, il bâillait; il se retournait tellement que sa femme s'en inquiéta et lui demanda s'il était malade. 'Non, ma chère, mais il me semble que j'ai faim, et je songeais à cette poularde de Bresse si blanchette, si joliette, qu'on nous a presentée à diner, et à laquelle, cependant, nous avons fait un si mauvais accueil.'— 'S'il faut te dire ma confession, je t'avouerai mon ami, que j'ai tout autant d'appétit que toi, et puisque tu as songé à la poularde, il faut la faire venir et la manger.'— 'Quelle folie! tout dort dans la maison, et demain on se moquera de nous.'—'Si tout dort, tout se réveillera, et on ne se moquera pas de nous, parce qu'on n'en saura rien. Dailleurs, qui sait si d'ici à demain l'un de nous ne mourra pas de faim? Je ne veux pas en courir la chance. Je vais sonner Justine.'

Aussitôt dit, aussitôt fait; et on éveilla la pauvre soubrette, qui, ayant bien soupé, dormait comme on dort à dix-neuf ans, quand l'amour ne tourmente pas.

Elle arriva tout en désordre, les yeux bouffis, bâillant et s'assit en étendant les bras.

Mais ce n'était là qu'une tâche facile; il s'agissait d'avoir la cuisinière, et ce fut un affaire. Celle-ci était cordon bleu et partant souverainement rechigneuse; elle grondit, hennit, grogna, rugit et renâcla; cependant elle se leva à la fin, et cette circonstance enorme commença à se mouvoir.

Sur ces entrefaites, Madame de Versy avait passé une camisole, son mari s'était arrangé tant bien que mal, Justine avait étendu sur le lit une nappe, et apporté les accessoires indispensables d'un festin improvisé.

Tout étant ainsi préparé, on vit paraître la poularde, qui fut à l'instant dépecée et avalée sans misericorde.

Après ce premier exploit les époux se partagèrent une grosse poire de Saint-Germain, et mangèrent un peu de confiture d'oranges.

Dans les entr'actes, ils avaient creusé jusqu'au fond une bouteille de vin de Graves, et répeté plusieurs fois avec variation, qu'ils n'avaient jamais fait un plus agréable repas.

Ce repas finit pourtant. Justine ôta le couvert, fit disparaître les pièces de conviction, regagna son lit, et le rideau conjugal tomba sur les convives.

Le lendemain matin Madame de Versy courut chez son amie Madame de Franval et lui raconta tout ce qui s'était passé, et c'est à l'indiscrétion de celle-ci que le public doit la présente confidence.

Elle ne manquait jamais de remarquer qu'en finissant son récit, Madame de Versy avait toussé deux fois et rougi très-positivement.

BRILLAT-SAVARIN, *La Physiologie du Goût*.

THE NUPTIAL FEAST OF
JANUARY AND MAY

AND NOW the palace gates are open'd wide,
The guests appear in order, side by side,
And placed in state, the bridegroom and the bride.
The breathing flutes' soft notes are heard around
And the shrill trumpets mix their silver sound . . .

The beauteous dame sate smiling at the board,
And darted amorous glances at her Lord;
Not Hester's self whose charms the Hebrews sing,
E'er looked so lovely on her Persian King. . .

The joyful Knight survey'd her by his side
Nor envy'd Paris with the Spartan bride:
Still as his mind revolv'd with vast delight
Th'entrancing raptures of th'approaching night:
Restless he sate, invoking ev'ry power
To speed his bliss and haste the happy hour.
Meantime the vig'rous dancers beat the ground
And songs were sung and flowing bowls went round,
With od'rous spices they perfumed the place
And mirth and pleasure shone in ev'ry face. . .

The weary sun, as learned Poets write,
Forsook th'horizon and rolled down the light . . .

Then rose the guests and as the time required
Each paid his thanks, and decently retired. . .

The foe once gone, our Knight prepar'd t'undress
So keen he was, and eager to possess:
But first thought fit th'assistance to receive,
Which grave Physicians scruple not to give;

Satyrion near, with hot Eringo's stood,
Cantharides, to fire the lazy blood . . .

By this the sheets were spread, the bride undress'd,
The room was sprinkl'd, and the bed was bless'd.
What next ensued beseems not me to say;
'Tis sung he labour'd till the dawning day.

>   POPE, *January and May.*

VÉNUS AURA SON TOUR

VÉNUS aura son tour... Une table est servie...
Céphise, d'un vin blanc qu'elle aime à la folie,
Arrose quatre fois une aile de perdrix:
Des legers entremets dont les piquans esprits
Eveillent la vigeur de l'amoureux Athlète,
Poissons voluptueux, occupent mainte assiette...

Céphise en est prodigue; et l'adroit Cuisinier
Une fois averti, sait faire son métier.
Vers la fin du repas, de sa liqueur vermeille,
Beaune, Nuits ou Pomard fournit une bouteille—
Le nectar fait miracle: on se sent de l'esprit
On babille, on se lorgne, on s'agace, on sourit,
Deux bouches tour à tour ont mordue cette poire;
Après le Jouvenceau que Céphise vient de boire;
Quatre genoux mêlés s'embarrassent exprès...

Le désir... Il est temps de se voir de plus près...

Un lit voluptueux, decoré par la mode,
Offre dans l'autre pièce un théâtre commode.
Dieux! que Céphise est belle en cornette de nuit!

ANDRÉA DE NERÇIAT, *Contes Nouveaux*.

THE FOOD OF LOVE

THE APHRODISIACS of the Greek and Roman courtesans were made of pepper, myrrh and equal quantities of two scents called Cyprus and Egyptian, and ... the cups from which these potions were drunk were made of scented earthenware. According to Pliny the glands of animals were commonly used, especially those of the pig, the stag, the horse and the hyena...

Shakespeare attributes Othello's power over Desdemona to

> *... conjuration and mighty magic*
> *Thou hast practisèd on her with foul charms,*
> *Abused her delicate youth with drugs or minerals*
> *That weaken motion.*

The roots of the sea holly had a reputation as a love tonic ... in Queen Elizabeth's day, and a confection of these eryngo roots mixed with sugar became popular under the name of 'Kissing comfits' ...

During the Renaissance ... books were published containing recipes with curious and often revolting ingredients for inspiring amorous passions. The blood of a red-haired person, the obscene parts of animals, the hearts and tongues of toads and vipers, and the blood of a bat, were not unusual components. A very common ingredient was hippomanes (the thin membranes sometimes found covering the head of a newly born colt).

> *Then hippomanes for shepherds call it so*
> *Distil as venom from their parts below,*

> *Hippomanes that wicked stepdames pluck*
> *Mingling with herbs that bring bad luck.*

Hoffman's water of magnanimity... was said to contain winged ants macerated in alcohol...

The references in plays of the seventeenth and eighteenth centuries are probably to cantharides.

> *Straight to the 'pothecary's shop I went*
> *And in love powder all my money spent;*
> *Behap what will, next Sunday after prayers*
> *When to the ale house Lubberkin repairs,*
> *Then flies into his mug I'll throw*
> *And soon the swain with fervent love shall glow.*
>
> GAY.

There are many stories in history... of the terrible effects of this drug... The aphrodisiac properties are seldom induced unless the dose is big enough to endanger life... as in the story quoted by Ramsey (1663) of the courtesan who prepared a magnificent supper for an infatuated young man at which every dish was flavoured with cantharides, from the results of which he died the following day...

Madame de Pompadour, who resorted to a tincture of cantharides when she thought she was losing the love of Louis XV, was rescued by the Duchess de Brancas, who, finding the bottle, and recognizing the smell of the contents, threw it up the chimney, leaving the king's mistress to her less harmful diet of 'chocolat à triple vanille' and celery soup, a 'régime un peu échauffant,' ... prescribed to correct her naturally cold temperament...

Alcohol sweetened with sugar is a common French restorative, and, it is said, was first invented to increase the ardour of the aged King Louis XIV. It is still a custom in some countries to give a bride and bridegroom cakes moistened with sugar and alcohol on their wedding night... In Persia newly-married couples are given sheep's trotters steeped in vinegar... Ambergris is regarded in the East to-day as a potent aphrodisiac, and coffee is served in cups with a hollow drilled in the bottom to contain a piece of ambergris... A tincture of ambergris was a very usual addition to tea and coffee in the seventeenth century... 'You may talk,' said Ravenscroft (1622), 'of your amber caudles, your chocolate and jelly broths, but they are nothing comparable to youth and beauty.'

MRS. LEYEL, *The Magic of Herbs*.

III: THE PHILOSOPHY OF FOOD

My Reason is my Friend, yours is a Cheat:
Hunger calls out, my Reason bids me eat;
Perversly yours, your Appetite does mock;
This asks for food, that answers what's a Clock.

ROCHESTER.

CHARACTERISTICS OF THE GOURMET

THEY have broad faces, sparkling eyes, small foreheads, short noses, full lips and round chins. The females are plump, rather pretty than handsome, with a tendency to *embonpoint*. It is under this exterior that the pleasantest guests are to be found: they accept all that is offered, eat slowly and taste with reflection. They never hurry away from the places where they have been well treated; and you are sure of them for the evening, because they know all the games and pastimes which form the ordinary accessories of a gastronomic meeting.

Those on the contrary to whom nature has refused an aptitude for the enjoyment of taste, have long faces, long noses, and large eyes; whatever their height they have always in their *tournure* a character of elongation. They have black and straight hair, and are above all, deficient in *embonpoint*: it is they who invented trousers. The women whom nature has afflicted with the same misfortune are angular, get tired at table, and live on tea and scandal.

BRILLAT-SAVARIN, *La Physiologie du Goût*.

'DOTH A MAN THAT IS ADRY DESIRE TO DRINK IN GOLD?'

A POOR MAN takes more delight in an ordinary meal's meat, which he hath but seldom, than they do with all their exotic dainties and continual viands; 'tis the rarity and necessity that makes a thing acceptable and pleasant. Darius, put to flight by Alexander, drank puddle water to quench his thirst; and it was pleasanter, he swore, than any wine or mead. All excess, as Epictetus argues, will cause a dislike; sweet will be sour, which made that temperate Epicurus sometimes voluntarily fast. But they, being always accustomed to the same dishes (which are nastily dressed by slovenly cooks, that after their obscenities never wash their bawdy hands) be they fish, flesh, compounded, made dishes, or whatsoever else, are therefore cloyed; nectar's self grows loathsome to them, they are weary of all their fine palaces, they are to them but as so many prisons. A poor man drinks in a wooden dish, and eats his meat in wooden spoons, wooden platters, earthen vessels, and such homely stuff: the other in gold, silver, and precious stones; but with what success? . . . fear of poison in the one, security in the other. . .

Cleopatra hath whole boars and sheep served up to her table at once, drinks jewels dissolved, 40,000 sesterces in value, but to what end?

Num tibi cum fauces urit sitis, aurea quaeris Pocula?

Doth a man that is adry desire to drink in gold?

BURTON, *The Anatomy of Melancholy.*

GOURMANDISE

GOURMANDISE is by no means unbecoming in women; it agrees with the delicacy of their organs, and serves to compensate them for some pleasures from which they are obliged to abstain, and for some evils to which nature appears to have condemned them. Nothing is more pleasant than to see a pretty *gourmande* under arms: her napkin is nicely adjusted; one of her hands is rested on the table; the other conveys to her mouth little morsels elegantly carved, or the wing of a partridge which it is necessary to pick; her eyes are sparkling, her lips glossy, her conversation, all her movements gracious; she is not devoid of that spice of *coquetterie* which women infuse into everything. With so many advantages she is irresistible; and Cato the Censor himself would yield to the influence. 'The penchant of the fair sex for *gourmandise* has in it somewhat of the nature of instinct, for *gourmandise* is favourable to beauty. A train of exact and rigid observations have demonstrated that a succulent, delicate, and careful regimen repels to a distance, and for a length of time, the external appearances of old age. It gives more brilliancy to the eyes, more freshness to the skin, more support to the muscles; and as it is certain in physiology that it is the depression of the muscles which causes wrinkles, those formidable enemies of beauty, it is equally true to say that . . . those who understand eating are comparatively ten years younger than those who are strangers to this science. . .

Again *gourmandise*, when partaken, has the most marked influence on the happiness of the conjugal state.

A wedded pair endowed with this taste have once a day, at least, an agreeable cause of meeting. Music, no doubt, has powerful attractions for those who love it; but it is necessary to set about it, it is an exertion. Moreover, one may have a cold, the music is not at hand, the instruments are out of tune, one has the blue devils, or it is a day of rest. In *gourmandise*, on the contrary, a common want summons the pair to table; the same inclination retains them there; they naturally practise towards one another those little attentions which show a wish to oblige; and the manner in which their meals are conducted enters materially into the happiness of life.

BRILLAT-SAVARIN, *La Physiologie du Goût*.

'HE DINES UNSCATHED WHO DINES ALONE'

(Madame du Deffand to Horace Walpole.)

Paris, 1768 ...

MES SOUPERS DE DIMANCHES sont déplorables, j'en faisais hier la réflexion; je me tourment pour avoir du monde, nous étions douze, il n'y avait personne que j'écoutasse ni dont j'eusse envie de me faire écouter, et cependant je l'avoue, j'aime mieux cela que d'être seule.

The Letters of Mme. du Deffand to Horace Walpole.

JUVENAL'S FIFTH SATIRE

[Note: Juvenal's Fifth Satire describes a dinner party at which Virro, the patron, eats and drinks of the best, while Trebius, the parasite, is insulted by the servants, and starved upon bad food.]

FOR FIRST, of this be sure, whene'er your lord
Thinks proper to invite you to his board,
He pays, or thinks he pays, the total sum
Of all your pains, past, present, and to come . . .

If, after two long months, he condescend
To waste a thought upon a humble friend,
Reminded by a vacant seat, and write,
'You, Master Trebius, sup with me to-night.' . . .

Before your patron cups of price are placed,
Amber and gold, with rows of beryls graced:
Cups you can only at a distance view,
And never trusted to such a guest as you! . . .

If Virro's veins with indigestion glow,
They bring him water cooled in Scythian snow:
What! Did I late complain a different wine
Fell to thy share? A different water's thine!
Getulian slaves your vile potations pour,
Or the coarse paws of some huge, raw-boned Moor,
Whose hideous form the stoutest would affray,
If met, by moonlight, near the Latian way:
On him, a youth, the flower of Asia waits,
So dearly purchased that the joint estates
Of Tullus, Ancus, would not yield the sum,
Nor all the wealth of all the Kings of Rome! . . .

Mark with what insolence another thrusts
Before your plate, th'impenetrable crusts,

Black, mouldy, fragments which defy the saw,
The mere despair of every aching jaw!...

But lo! a lobster introduced in state
Stretches, enormous, o'er the bending plate!
Proud of a length of tail, he seems to eye
The humbler guests with scorn, as towering by,
He takes the place of honour at the board,
And, crowned with costly pickles, greets his lord!
A crab is yours, ill-garnished, and ill-fed,
With half an egg—a supper for the dead!
  He pours Venafran oil upon his fish,
While the stale coleworts in your wooden dish
Stink of the lamp; for such to you is thrown
Such rancid grease as Africk sends to town;...

  Vain hope! Near him a goose's liver lies,
A capon equal to a goose in size;
A boar, too, smokes, like that which fell, of old,
By the famed hero, with the locks of gold.
Last, if the spring its genial influence shed
And welcome thunders call them from their bed,
Large mushrooms enter: Ravish'd with their size,
  'O Libya, keep thy grain!' Alledius cries,
And bid thy oxen to their stalls retreat,
Nor, while thou grow'st such mushrooms think of wheat!'
  Meanwhile, to put your patience to the test,
Lo! the spruce carver to his task addrest,
Skips, like a harlequin, from place to place,
And waves his knife with pantomimick grace,
Till every dish be ranged, and every joint
Severed, by nicest rules, from point to point.
You think this folly—'tis a simple thought—

To such perfection, now, is carving brought,
That different gestures, by our curious men,
Are used for different dishes, hare and hen...

  You champ on spongy toadstools, hateful treat!
Fearful of poison in each bite you eat:
He feasts secure on mushrooms fine as those
Which Claudius for his special eating chose,
Till one more fine, provided by his wife,
Finished at once, his feasting, and his life!

  Apples as fragrant and as bright of hue
As those which in Alcinous' gardens grew,
Mellowed by constant sunshine; or as those
Which graced the Hesperides in burnished rows;
Apples which you may smell, but never taste,
Before your lord and his great friends are placed:
While you enjoy mere windfalls; such stale fruit
As serves to mortify the raw recruit...

Your palate still beguiles you! Ah, how nice
That smoking haunch! Now we shall have a slice!
Now that half hare is coming! Now a bit
Of that young pullet! Now—and thus you sit,
Thumbing your bread in silence; watching still
For what has never reached you, never will!

  No more of freedom! 'Tis a vain pretence:
Your patron treats you like a man of sense.
For if you can, without a murmur, bear,
You well deserve the insults which you share.
Anon, like voluntary slaves, you'll throw
Your humbled necks beneath the oppressor's blow,
Nay, with bare backs, solicit to be beat,
And merit SUCH A FRIEND, and SUCH A TREAT!

      JUVENAL, *Satires* (trans: by Gifford).

DELICATE HUMANITY

HE [Johnson] honoured me with his company at dinner on the 16th of October, at my lodgings in Old Bond Street, with Sir Joshua Reynolds, Mr. Garrick, Dr. Goldsmith, Mr. Murphy, Mr. Bickerstaff, and Mr. Thomas Davies. Garrick played round him with a fond vivacity, taking hold of the breasts of his coat, and, looking up in his face with a lively archness, complimented him on the good health he seemed to enjoy; while the sage, shaking his head beheld him with a gentle complacency. One of the company not being come at the appointed hour, I proposed, as usual, upon such occasions, to order dinner to be served; adding, 'Ought six people to be kept waiting for one?' 'Why, yes,' answered Johnson, with a delicate humanity, 'if the one will suffer more by your sitting down, than the six will do by waiting.'

BOSWELL, *Life of Samuel Johnson*.

A GREAT AND GOOD MAN

A YOUTH, invited to spend a whole holiday at Holland House, was told that he might have what he liked for dinner. Wise beyond his years, he chose duck and green peas, with an apricot tart to follow. 'My boy,' said Lord Holland, 'if in all the important questions of your life you decide as wisely as you have decided now, you will be a great and good man.'

SANDERS, *The Holland House Circle*.

'GOD HELP THE WICKED'

OH! That second Bottle is the Sincerest, Wisest, and most Impartial, Downright Friend we have; tells us truth of ourselves, and forces us to speak Truths of Others; banishes Flattery from our Tongues, and distrust from our Hearts; sets us above the mean Policy of Court Prudence; which makes us lie to one another all Day, for fear of being betrayed by each other at Night. And ... I believe, the errantest Vilain breathing, is honest as long as that Bottle lives, and few of that Tribe dare venture upon him, at least among the Courtiers and Statesmen.

Rochester-Savile Correspondance.

A GOOD APPETITE THE BEST SAUCE

WHAT, and how great, the Virtue and the Art
To live on little with a cheerful heart
(A Doctrine sage, but truly none of mine),
Let's talk my friends, but talk before we dine:
Not when a gilt Buffet's reflected pride
Turns you from sound Philosophy aside;
Not when from Plate to Plate your eyeballs roll,
And the brain dances to the mantling bowl . . .

Go work, hunt, exercise! (he thus began)
Then scorn a homely dinner if you can.
Your wine locked up, your Butler strolled abroad,
Or kept from fish (the River yet un-thaw'd)
If then plain bread and milk will do the feat
The pleasure lies in you, not in the meat.
Preach as I please, I doubt our curious men
Will chuse a Pheasant still before a Hen;
Yet Hens of Guinea full as good I hold,
Except you eat the feathers green and gold.
Of Carps and Mullets, why prefer the great,
(Tho' cut in pieces e'er my Lord can eat),
Yet for small Turbots such esteem profess?
Because God made these large, the other less.
Oldfield, with more than happy throat endu'd
Cries, 'Send me Gods! a whole Hog barbecu'd!'
Oh blast it, South winds, till a stench exhale
Rank as the ripeness of a Rabbit's tail
By what Criterion do ye eat, d'ye think,
If this is prized for sweetness, that for stink?
When the tired Glutton labours thro' a Treat

He'll find no relish in the sweetest Meat,
He calls for something bitter, something sour,
And the rich feast concludes extremely poor;
Cheap eggs, and herbs, and herbs, and olives, still we see,
This much is left of old Simplicity!
  The robin-red-breast till of late had rest,
And children sacred held a Martin's nest
Till Becca-ficos sold so devilish dear,
To one that was, or would have been, a Peer.
Let me extoll a Cat on Oysters fed,
I'll have a Party at the Bedford Head,
Or even to crack live Crawfish recommend
I'd never doubt at Court to make a friend! . . .

Between Excess and Famine lies a mean,
Plain, but not sordid, tho' not splendid, clean.
Avidien and his Wife (no matter which
For him you'll call a dog, and her a bitch)
Sell their presented Partridges and Fruits,
And humbly live on Rabbits and on Roots:
One half-pint bottle serves them both to dine,
And is at once their vinegar and wine. . .

  He knows to live who keeps the middle state
And neither leans on this side or on that:
Nor stops for one bad Cork his Butler's pay,
Swears, like Albutius, a good Cook away;
Nor lets, like Naevius, every error pass,
The measly wine, foul cloth, or greasy glass.

　　POPE, *Imitations of the Satires of Horace*.

IV: GASTRONOMIC ODDITIES

'Tis the dessert that graces all the feast,
For an ill end disparages the rest:
Make your transparent sweet-meats timely rise,
With Indian sugar, and Arabian spice;
And let your various creams enriched be
With swelling fruit just ravished from the tree.

Apician Morsels.

DESSERT

HORACE WALPOLE says: The last branch of our fashion into which the close observation of nature has been introduced, is our dessert. Jellies, biscuits, sugar-plums, and creams, have long given way to harlequins, gondoliers, Turks, Chinese, and shepherdesses of Saxon china. But these, unconnected, and only seeming to wander among groves of curled paper and silk flowers, were soon discovered to be too insipid and unmeaning. By degrees meadows of cattle of the same brittle materials spread themselves over the table; cottages rose in sugar, and temples in barley-sugar; pigmies, Neptunes, in cars of cockle shells, triumphed over oceans of looking-glass or seas of silver tissue. Women of the first quality came home from Chevenix's laden with dolls and babies, not for their children, but for their housekeeper. At last even these puerile puppet-shows are sinking into disuse, and more manly ways of concluding our repasts are established. Gigantic figures succeed to pigmies; and it is known that a celebrated confectioner (Lord Albemarle's) complained that, after having prepared a middle dish of gods and goddesses eighteen feet high, his lord would not cause the ceiling of his parlour to be demolished to facilitate their entry. '*Imaginez-vous,*' said he, '*que Milord n'a pas voulu ôter le plafond!*'

LORD ORFORD, *Works.*

LES FANTAISIES GASTRONOMIQUES
DE LUNÉVILLE

LE ROI STANISLAS dépensait des sommes considérables pour sa table; elle n'était pas seulement servie avec profusion et raffinement, mais il l'entourait d'un luxe inouï. Il fait imiter les fontaines monumentales de Nancy et des véritables jets d'eau surgissent sur les tables pendant les repas.

Stanislas était un véritable gastronome et les plaisirs de la table formaient l'une de ses distractions favourites. Il était, du reste, douée d'appetit si violent qu'il avançait souvent l'heure de son dîner: 'Pour peur que votre Majesté continue (lui disait un jour Monsieur G.) elle finira par dîner la veille!'

Son goût n'était pas toujours exquis: ainsi il mangeait sans cuisson la choucroute ou des choux râpés saupoudrés de sucre, et des viandes cuites avec des fruits. 'C'étaient surtout les desserts qui étaient l'objet de sa sollicitude. Le chef d'office, un artiste nommé Joseph Gilliers, avait l'art de composer des desserts, des pièces montées qui faisaient la joie de Stanislas. Tantôt un jardin enchanté, tantôt 'au milieu d'un parc en miniature s'élève une grotte en rocaille, du sommet de laquelle jaillit une fontaine. Des promeneurs, figurés par des statuettes, semblent parcourir ces lieux charmants; d'autres y goûtent les douceurs du repos au milieu des fruits, des fleurs, et des sucreries.'

Les patisseries du Roi se livraient au plus ingénieuses fantaisies. Un jour quatre servants déposèrent sur la table royale un pâté monstre ayant la forme d'une citadelle. Tout à coup le couvercle se soulève et, des flancs du pâté, s'élance Bébé, la nain du Roi, costumé en guerrier, le casque en tête, un pistolet à la main qu'il fait partir au grand effroi des dames.

Mais le plaisir du monarque ne se bornait pas à servir à ses convives des plats récherchés; son plus grand bonheur était de truquer les mets et de jouir de leur crédulité ou de leur déception. Il faisait servir comme gibier étranger des oies plumées vivantes, tuées à coup de baguettes et marinées. Des dindons traités de la même manière, et marinés dans des herbes odoriférantes des bois, étaient présentés commes coqs de bruyère; et la joie du Roi était complète quand ses convives étaient dupes de ces inventions.

MAUGRAS, *La Cour de Lunéville au XVIIIme siècle*.

ROMAN LUXURIES

AMONG the luxuries of the table in greatest request, Gellius quotes out of Varro, the peacock from Samos, the Phrygian turkey, cranes from Melos, Ambracian kids, the Tartesian mullet, trouts from Persenumtium, Tarentine oysters, crabs from Chios, Tatian nuts, Egyptian dates, Iberian chestnuts; all of which institutions of bills of fare were invented for the wicked wantonness of luxury and gluttony...

Albinus, who ruled in Gaul, devoured at one supper one hundred peaches, ten melons, fifty large green figs, and three hundred oysters. And Maximus, the emperor, who succeeded Alexander Memmeas, consumed forty pounds of flesh in one day, and drank an amphora of wine, containing forty-eight quarts. Geta, the emperor, was also a prodigious epicure, causing his dishes to be brought in alphabetically, and would continue feeding for three days together...

Vitellius, according to Suetonius, had a supper, where two thousand rare, and foreign, fishes were presented upon the table, with other strange birds, brought from the Straits of Gibraltar by galleys, sent on purpose to transport them to Rome...

It is said, that Papirius Petus was the patron of custard; that the Tetrapharmacon, a dish much admired by the emperors Adrian and Alexander Severus, was made of pheasant, peacock, a wild sow's hock and udder, with a bread pudding over it; and that the name & reason of so odd a dish are to be sought for among the physicians...

Heliogabalus had the peculiar glory of first making sausages of shrimps, crabs, oysters, prawns, and lobsters.

Æsop had a supper of the tongues of birds that could speak; and his daughter regaled on pearls, though he does not tell us how she dressed them; Hortensius left ten thousand pipes of wine in his cellar for his heir's drinking; Vedius Pollio fed his fish-ponds with human flesh; and Cæsar bought ten thousand weight of lampreys for his triumphal supper . . .

The most exquisite animal was reserved for the last chapter, and that was the dormouse, a harmless creature, whose innocence might at least have defended it from cooks and physicians. But Apicius found out an odd sort of fate for these poor creatures—some to be boned, others to be put whole with odd ingredients, into hogs' guts, and so boiled for sausages. In ancient times people made it their business to fatten them. Aristotle rightly observes that sleep fattened them; and Martial, too, poetically tells us that sleep was their only nourishment. But the annotator has cleared up that point; he, good man, has tenderly observed one of them for many years, and finds that it does not sleep all the winter, as falsely recorded, but wakes at meals, and after its repast rolls itself up in a ball to sleep.

This dormouse, according to the author, did not drink in three years time; but whether other dormice do so is not known, because Bambouselbergius's treatise of the mode of fattening dormice is lost. Though very costly, they became a common diet of great entertainments. Petronius delivers us an odd receipt for dressing them, and serving them up with poppies and honey which must be a very soporiferous dainty, and as good as owl-pie to such as want a nap after dinner.

Apician Morsels. Anon.

GOOD HOUSEKEEPING—1665

THESE were the days wherein were practised the triumphs and trophies of cookery. One of these triumphs is the construction of a ship of confectionery, with guns charged with actual powder, and a castle of pies containing live frogs and birds. After the firing of the guns the ladies are advised to 'take the eggshells full of sweet waters and throw them at each other. All dangers being seemingly over, by this time you may suppose they will desire to see what is in the pyes; where, lifting first the lid off one pye, out skip some frogs, which makes the ladies to skip and shreek; next after, the other pye, whence come out the birds, who, by a natural instinct, flying in the light will put out the candles; so that, what with the flying birds and skipping frogs, the one above, the other beneath, will cause much delight and pleasure to the whole company: at length the candles are lighted and a banquet brought in, the musick sounds and everyone with much delight and content rehearses their actions in the former passages.' These were the delights of the nobility before good housekeeping left England.

MAY, *The Accomplisht Cook.*

'TO IMITATE IN SUCH A MANNER IS TO CREATE'

A RICH PATRICIAN brought up with tender care a young chef de cuisine, whom his major domo had bequeathed to him on his death-bed, as Mazarin did Colbert to Louis XIV.

One day some guests of the highest class met together at the residence of the noble Amphitryon, who often claimed the authority of their enlightened judgement. The learned Areopagitæ had to pronounce on certain new dishes: it was necessary by dint of seduction, to captivate the favour and patronage of these judges ...

Everything was served to the greatest nicety, and they only awaited the dessert—that little course which causes the emotion of the great culinary drama to be forgotten—when the young chef appeared and placed in the centre of the table a silver dish containing twelve eggs. 'Eggs!' exclaimed the host. The astonished guests looked at each other in silence. The cook took one of the eggs, placed it in a little china boat, slightly broke the shell, and begged his master to taste the contents. The latter continued to remove the white envelope, and at length discovered a savoury and perfumed ball of fat. It was a fig-pecker of a golden colour—fat, delicate, exquisite—surrounded by a wonderful seasoning. The good old man cast on his pupil a look full of tenderness and pride ... 'You are inspired by Petronius,' said he, 'to imitate in such a manner is to create.'

SOYER, *Pantropheon*.

NAPOLEON'S COOKS

'WHO can combine goût with new combinations? 'Tis yourself Leander.' . . . 'What you learned from me came at least from a good school. It is something to have served under Napoleon,' added Prevost, with the grand air of the Imperial Kitchen. 'Had it not been for Waterloo I should have had the Cross. But the Bourbons and the Cooks of the Empire never could understand each other. They brought over an imigrant chef who did not comprehend the taste of the age. He wished to bring everything back to the time of the œil de bœuf. When Napoleon passed my soup of Austerlitz untasted I knew the old family was doomed.'

DISRAELI, *Tancred.*

FOIE GRAS

WE ALL THREE once more entered the *fiacre*, and drove to the celebrated restaurateur's of the Rue Mont Orgueil. O, blissful recollections of that dinner! ... Lonely and sorrowful as I now sit, digesting with many a throe the iron thews of a British beefsteak ... I see the grateful apparitions of *Escallopes de Saumon* and *Laitances de Carpes* rise in a gentle vapour before my eyes... And thou most beautiful of all, thou evening star of *entremets*—thou that delightest in truffles, and gloriest in a dark cloud of sauces—exquisite *foie gras*!—Have I forgotten thee? Do I not, on the contrary, see thee, smell thee, taste thee, and almost die with rapture of thy possession? What though the goose, of which thou art a part, has, indeed, been roasted alive by a slow fire, in order to increase thy divine proportions—yet has not our almanach truly declared that the goose rejoiced amid all her tortures ... because of the glory that awaited her? Did she not, in prophetic vision, behold her enlarged and ennobled *foie* dilate into *patés* and steam into *sautés*—the companion of truffles—the glory of dishes—the delight—the treasure—the transport of gourmands! O, exalted among birds—the apotheosised goose, did not thy heart exult even when thy liver parched and swelled within thee, from that most agonising death; and didst thou not, like the Indians at the stake, triumph in the very torments which alone could render thee illustrious?

LORD LYTTON, *Pelham*

GASTRONOMIC ECCENTRICITIES

WE MUST beg pardon of the reader for informing him that the dog presented a very relishing dish to many nations advanced in culinary science. To them, one of these animals, young, plump, and delicately prepared, appeared excellent food. The Greeks (we grieve to say) ate dogs, and even dared to think them good: the grave Hippocrates himself—the most wise, the least gluttonous, and therefore the most impartial of their physicians—was convinced that this quadruped furnished a wholesome, and at the same time, a light, food. As to the Romans, they also liked it, and no doubt prepared it in the same manner as the hare, which they thought it resembled in taste.

Atheneus, describing a feast of the most exquisite elegance, names double tripe among a host of dishes. He also says, speaking of a state dinner, that first of all there appeared large basins containing the intestines of animals, disposed with art around their heads.

At Rome the peacock had a prodigious success. When alive the Romans praised its beauty: when dead it appeared on the tables of its enthusiastic admirers. Ultimately more savoury or more rare dishes took the place of peacock's flesh, which then began to be thought hard, unwholesome, and of difficult digestion. However, it re-appeared in the Middle Ages at the nuptial festivities of the rich, where one of these birds was served as if alive, with the beak and claws gilded. To do that well, it was necessary to skin the bird very carefully, and then cook it with aromatics, such as cinnamon, cloves, etc. It was then covered with its skin and feathers, and served without any appearance of having been stripped. This luxury was to gratify the sight. Nobody touched it. The peacock was thus preserved for several years without being damaged—a property believed to be peculiar to its flesh, but which was owing no doubt to the aromatics just mentioned...

Certain wandering tribes of Asia and Africa were thought formerly to be very fond of grilled elephant.

In our days also some semi-savage nations partake of the same taste. Le Vaillant, a celebrated traveller, and a most distinguished gastronomist, tells us that the first time he partook of an elephant's trunk, which was served him by the Hottentots, he resolved that it should not be the last; for nothing appeared to him of a more exquisite flavour. But he reserves his greatest praises for the foot of the colossal quadruped. We will let him speak for himself:—'They cut off the four feet of the animal, and made in the earth a hole about three feet square. This was filled with live charcoal, and, covering the hole with very dry wood, a large fire was kept up during part of the night. When they thought that the hole was hot enough it was emptied: a Hottentot then placed within it the four feet of the animal, covered them with hot ashes, and then with charcoal and small wood; and this fire was left burning until the morning... My servants presented me at breakfast with an elephant's foot. It had considerably swelled in the cooking; I could hardly recognise the shape, but it appeared so good, exhaled so inviting an odour, that I hastened to taste it. I could not conceive how so heavy, so material, an animal as the elephant, could furnish a dish so fine and delicate, and I devoured without bread, my elephant's foot, while my Hottentots, seated around me, regaled themselves with other parts which they found equally delicious.

The Romans never evinced fondness for the flesh of the elephant. This animal, with its gigantic proportions and rare intelligence, was found to be so amusing to the nation of kings, when dancing on the tightrope, or in the terrible combats of the circus, that they hardly thought of roasting it, or making it into fricassees. We cannot, however, affirm that the gastronomic eccentricity of some Roman epicure did not dream of a monstrous feast in which he may have offered to his guests an elephant *à la Troyenne* on a silver dish made purposely for the occasion!

Heliogabalus, who understood good living, contented himself with the brains of ostriches. Six hundred of these animals furnished enough for one meal. The devastation was great, but the Emperor had made a good supper.

The red mullet, which is still much esteemed, was considered one of the most delicate of dishes, and the Romans in fashionable circles employed it in a refinement of pleasure of a singular kind. It is well known that this fish, when the scales are removed, still remains of a fine pink colour. The fops of Rome having remarked that at the death this colour passed through a succession of the most beautiful shades, the poor mullet was served alive, inclosed in a glass vessel; and the guests, attentive, and greedy of emotions, enjoyed this cruel spectacle which presented to them a gradation of colours which insensibly disappeared.

Crassus, who displayed so little tenderness towards his servants, had an extraordinary weakness concerning his fine sea-eels. He passed his life beside the superb fish-pond where he lovingly fattened them from his own hand. Ornamented with necklaces of the finest pearls, and earrings of precious stones, all, at a signal, swam towards him; several fearlessly took the food he offered them; and some allowed their master to caress them without seeking to bite or avoid him. It was a much more exciting spectacle to witness a swarm of sea-eels tearing to pieces an awkward or rebellious slave; besides, it greatly improved the fish. The atrocious Vedius Pollio, who understood these matters, never failed to have sea-eels served him after their odious repast, that he might have the pleasure of eating some part of the body of his victim.

SOYER, *Pantropheon*.

A MODEST PROPOSAL

I SHALL NOW therefore humbly propose my own thoughts, which I hope will not be liable to the least objection.

I have been assured by a very knowing American of my acquaintance in London, that a young healthy child, well nursed, is at a year old a most delicious, nourishing, and wholesome food, whether stewed, roasted, baked, or boiled; and I make no doubt that it will equally serve in a fricassee or a ragout.

I do therefore humbly offer it to public consideration, that of the hundred and twenty thousand children already computed, twenty thousand may be reserved for breed, whereof only one-fourth part to be males; which is more than we allow to sheep, black-cattle, or swine; and my reason is, that these children are seldom the fruits of marriage, a circumstance not much regarded by our savages, therefore one male will be sufficient to serve four females. That the remaining hundred thousand may, at a year old, be offered in sale to the persons of quality and fortune through the kingdom; always advising the mother to let them suck plentifully in the last month, as to render them plump and fat for a good table. A child will make two dishes at an entertainment for friends; and when the family dines alone, the fore or hind quarter will make a reasonable dish, and seasoned with a little pepper or salt, will be very good boiled on the fourth day, especially in winter.

I have reckoned, upon a medium, that a child just born will weigh twelve pounds and in a solar year, if tolerably nursed, will increase to twenty-eight pounds.

I grant this food will be somewhat dear, and therefore very proper for landlords, who, as they have already devoured most of the parents, seem to have the best title to the children.

Infant's flesh will be in season throughout the year, but more plentifully in March, and a little before and after: for we are told by a grave author, an eminent French physician, that fish being a prolific diet, there are more children born in Roman Catholic countries about nine months after Lent, than at any other season; therefore, reckoning a year after Lent, the markets will be more glutted than usual, because the number of popish infants is at least three to one in this kingdom; and therefore it will have one other collateral advantage by lessening the number of papists among us.

I have already computed the charge of nursing a beggar's child (in which list I reckon all cottagers, labourers, and four-fifths of the farmers) to be about two shillings per annum, rags included; and I believe no gentleman would repine to give ten shillings for the carcase of a good fat child, which, as I have said, will make four dishes of excellent nutritive meat, when he has only some particular friend or his own family to dine with him. Thus the squire will learn to be a good landlord, and grow popular among his tenants; the mother will have eight shillings neat profit, and be fit for work till she produces another child.

Those who are more thrifty (as I must confess the times require) may flay the carcase; the skin of which, artificially dressed, will make admirable gloves for ladies, and summer-boots for fine gentlemen.

As to our city of Dublin, shambles may be appointed for this purpose, in the most convenient parts of it, and butchers we may be assured will not be wanting; although I rather recommend buying the children alive, and dressing them hot from the knife, as we do roasting pigs...

I profess, in the sincerity of my heart, that I have not the least personal interest in endeavouring to promote this necessary work, having no other motive than the public good of my country, by advancing our trade, providing for infants, relieving the poor, and giving some pleasure to the rich. I have no children by which I can propose to get a single penny; the youngest being nine years old, and my wife past child-bearing.

SWIFT, *A Modest Proposal*.

THACKERAY ON SWIFT'S PROPOSAL

MR. DEAN ... enters the nursery with tread and gaiety of an ogre. 'I have been assured', says he in the "Modest Proposal," 'by a very knowing American of my acquaintance in London, that a young healthy child, well nursed, is, at a year old, a most delicious, nourishing, and wholesome food, whether stewed, roasted, baked, or boiled; and I make no doubt it will equally serve in a ragout.' And taking up this pretty joke, as his way is, he argues it with perfect gravity and logic. He turns and twists this subject in a score of different ways: he hashes it, he serves it up cold; and he garnishes it, and relishes it always. He describes the little animal as 'dropped from its dam', advising that the mother should let it suck plentifully in the last month, so as to render it plump and fat for a good table! 'A child', says his Reverence, 'will make two dishes at an entertainment for friends; and when the family dines alone, the fore or hind quarter will make a reasonable dish,' and so on, and the subject being so delightful that he can't leave it, he proceeds to recommend, in place of venison for squires' tables, 'the bodies of young lads and maidens not exceeding fourteen or under twelve.' Amiable humourist! laughing castigator of morals! There was a process well known and practised in the Dean's gay days: when a lout entered the coffee-house, the wags proceeded to what they called 'roasting' him. This is roasting a subject with a vengeance. The Dean had a naive genius for it. As the 'Almanach des Gourmands' says:—'*On nait rôtisseur.*'

THACKERAY, *The Four Georges.*

TO COLERIDGE

DEAR C.—It gives me great satisfaction to hear that the pig turned out so well—they are interesting creatures at a certain age—what a pity such buds should blow out into the maturity of rank bacon! You had all some of the crackling and brain sauce—did you remember to rub it with butter and gently dredge it a little just before the crisis? Did the eyes come away kindly with no Œdipean avulsion? Was the crackling the colour of the ripe pomegranate? Had you no complement of boiled neck of mutton before it, to blunt the edge of delicate desire? Did you flesh maiden teeth in it? Not that I sent the pig... To confess an honest truth, a pig is one of those things I could never think of sending away. Teals, widgeons, snipes, barndoor fowl, ducks, geese—your tame villatic things—Welsh mutton, collars of brawn, sturgeons, fresh or pickled, your potted char, Swiss cheeses, French pies, early grapes, muscadines, I impart as freely unto my friends as to myself. They are but self-extended... But pigs are pigs, and I myself therein am nearest to myself...

Yours (short of pig) to command in everything.

C. L.

LAMB, *Letters*.

A DAINTY ASSE

HOW *APULEIUS was sold to two brethren, whereof one was a Baker and the other a Cooke, and how finely and daintily he fared.*

When night came that Supper was done, and their business ended, they would bring many good morsels into their Chamber for themselves. One would bring Pigs, Chickens, Fish, and other good meates, the other fine bread, pasties, tarts, custards and other delicate Junkets dipped in hony. And when they had shut their Chamber doore, and went to the bains: (O Lord) how I would fill my guts with these goodly dishes: neither was I so much a foole, or so very an Asse, to leave the dainty meats, and to grind my teeth upon hard hay. In this sort I continued a great space, for I played the honest Asse, taking but a little of one dish, and a little of another, whereby no man distrusted me. In the end I was hardier and began to devour the whole messe of the sweet delicates, which caused the Baker and the Cooke to suspect, howbeit they nothing mistrusted me, but searched about to apprehend the theefe...

In the meane season, while I was fed with dainty morsels, I gathered together my flesh, my skin waxed soft, my hair began to shine, and was gallant on every part, but such faire and comely shape of my body, was cause of my dishonour, for the Baker and Cooke marvelled to see me so slick and fine considering I did eat no hay at all. Wherefore on a time at their accustomed houre, they went to the baines and locked their chamber doore. It fortuned that ere they departed away, they espied me through a hole, how I fell roundly to my victuals: then they marvelled greatly and little esteemed the loss of their meate...

Then I perceiving every man laugh, was nothing abashed, but rather more bold, whereby I never rested eating, till such time as the master of the house commanded me to be brought into his parler as a novelty, and there caused all kind of meates which were never touched to be set on the table, which I did greedily devour and made a cleane riddance of all the delicate meates. And to prove my nature wholly, they gave me such meates as every Asse doth abhorre: for they put before me beefe and vinegar, birds and pepper, fish and verjuice... Then one of the servants of the house said to his master, I pray you sir, give him some drink to his supper: Marry (quoth hee) I think thou saist true, for it may be that to his meate hee would drinke likewise a cup of wine. Hoe boy, wash yonder pot, and fill it with wine which done, carry it to the Asse, and say that I have drunke to him... But I (as soone as I beheld the cup) staied not long, but gathering my lips together, supped up all the wine at one draught. The master being right joyfull hereat caused the Baker and Cooke which had bought me to come before him, to whom he delivered four times as much for me as they paid.

APULEIUS, *The Golden Asse* (trans: by Adlington).

A BROKEN ENGAGEMENT

(From Miss C. Lutterell to Miss M. Lesley.)

Glenford, February 12th.

I HAVE A THOUSAND excuses to beg for having so long delayed thanking you my dear Peggy for your agreeable Letter, which believe me I should not have deferred doing, had not every moment of my time during the last five weeks been so fully employed in the necessary arrangements for my sister's wedding... And now what provokes me more than anything else is that the Match is broke off, and all my Labour thrown away. Imagine how great the Disappointment must be to me, when you consider that after having laboured both by Night and by Day, in order to get the Wedding dinner ready by the time appointed, after having roasted Beef, Broiled Mutton, and Stewed Soup enough to last the new-married Couple through the Honey-moon, I had the mortification of finding that I had been Roasting, Broiling and Stewing both the Meat and Myself to no purpose. Indeed, my dear Friend, I never remember suffering any vexation equal to what I experienced on last Monday when my sister came running to me in the store-room with her face as White as a Whipt Syllabub, and told me that Hervey had been thrown from his Horse, had fractured his Scull and was pronounced by his surgeon to be in the most emminent Danger. 'Good God! (said I) you don't say so? Why what in the name of Heaven will become of all the Victuals! We shall never be able to eat it while it is good. However, we'll call in the Surgeon to help us. I shall be able to manage the Sirloin myself, my Mother will eat the soup, and You and the Doctor must finish the rest.' Here I was interrupted, by seeing my poor Sister fall down to all appearance Lifeless upon one of the Chests, where we keep our table linen. I immediately called my Mother and the Maids, and at last we brought her to herself again ... we laid her upon the Bed, and she continued for some Hours in the most dreadful Convulsions. My Mother and I continued in the room with her, and when any intervals of tolerable Composure in Eloisa would allow us, we joined in heartfelt lamentations on the dreadful Waste in our provisions which the Event must occasion, and in concerting some plan for getting rid of them. We agreed that the best thing we could do was to begin eating them immediately, and accordingly we ordered up the cold Ham and Fowls, and instantly began our Devouring Plan on them with great Alacrity. We would have persuaded Eloisa to have taken a wing of Chicken, but she would not be persuaded... We endeavoured to rouse her by every means in our power, but to no purpose. I talked to her of Henry. 'Dear Eloisa (said I) there's no occasion for your crying so much about such a trifle. (For I was willing to make light of it in order to comfort her.) I beg you would not mind it—You see it does not vex me in the least; though perhaps *I* may suffer most from it after all; for I shall not only be obliged to eat up all the Victuals I have dressed already, but must if Henry should recover (which however is not very likely) dress as much for you again; or should he die (as I suppose he will) I shall still have to prepare a Dinner for you whenever you marry any one else... Yet I daresay he'll die soon, and then his pain will be over and you will be easy, whereas my Trouble will last much longer, for work as hard as I may, I am certain that the pantry cannot be cleared in less than a fortnight.'

JANE AUSTEN, *Lesley Castle*.

VEAL PIE

'WEAL PIE,' said Mr. Weller, soliloquising ... 'wery good thing is weal pie, when you know the lady as made it, and is quite sure it aint kittens; and arter all though, where's the odds, when they're so like weal that the wery piemen themselves don't know the difference?... I lodged in the same house as a pieman once, Sir, and a wery nice man he was, reg'lar clever chap too—make pies out o' anything, he could. 'What a number of cats you keep, Mr. Brooks,' says I, when I got intimate with him. 'Ah,' says he, 'I do—a good many,' says he. 'You must be wery fond of cats,' says I. 'Other people is,' says he a'winkin' at me, 'They an't in season till the winter though,' says he. 'Not in season!' says I. 'No,' says he, 'Fruits is in, cats is out,' 'Why, what do you mean?' says I. 'Mean,' says he, 'That I'll never be a party to the combination o' the butchers to keep up the prices of meat,' says he. 'Mr. Weller,' says he, a'squeezing my hand wery hard, and vispering in my ear—'Don't mention this here agin—but it's the seasoning as does it. They're all made of them noble animals,' says he, a'pointin' to a wery nice little tabby kitten, 'and I seasons 'em for beefsteak, weal, or kidney, 'cordin' to the demand. And more than that,' says he, 'I can make a weal a beefsteak, or a beefsteak a kidney, or any one on 'em a mutton, at a minute's notice, just as the market changes and appetites wary!'

DICKENS, *Pickwick Papers*.

A RECTORY BREAKFAST

AND NOW let us observe the well-furnished breakfast parlour at Plumstead Episcopi, and the comfortable air of all the belongings of the rectory. Comfortable they certainly were, but neither gorgeous nor even grand; indeed considering the money that had been spent there, the eye and taste might have been better served; there was an air of heaviness about the rooms which might have been avoided without any sacrifice of propriety; colours might have been better chosen and lights more perfectly diffused; but perhaps in doing so the thorough clerical aspect of the whole might have been somewhat marred. At any rate it was not without ample consideration that those thick, dark, costly carpets were put down; those embossed but sombre papers hung up; those heavy curtains draped so as to half exclude the light of the sun. Nor were these old-fashioned chairs, bought at a price far exceeding that now given for more modern goods, without a purpose. The breakfast service on the table was equally costly and equally plain. The apparent object had been to spend money without obtaining brilliancy or splendour. The urn was of thick and solid silver, as were also the tea-pot, coffee-pot, cream-ewer, and sugar-bowl; the cups were old, dim dragon china, worth about a pound a piece, but very despicable in the eyes of the uninitiated. The silver forks were so heavy as to be disagreeable to the hand, and the bread-basket was was of a weight really formidable to any but robust persons. The tea consumed was the very best, the coffee the very blackest, the cream the very thickest; there was dry toast and buttered toast, muffins and crumpets; hot bread and cold bread, white bread and brown bread, home-made bread and baker's bread, wheaten bread and oaten bread; and if there be other breads than these, they were there; there were eggs in napkins, and crispy bits of bacon under silver covers; and there were little fishes in a little box, and devilled kidneys frizzling on a hot-water dish;—which, by-the-by, were placed closely contiguous to the plate of the worthy archdeacon himself. Over and above this, on a snow white napkin, spread upon the side-board, was a huge ham and a huge sirloin; the latter having laden the dinner table on the previous evening. Such was the ordinary fare at Plumstead Episcopi.

TROLLOPE, *The Warden*.

THE OYSTERS

'THE KEEN AIR has given me an appetite,' said the dear angel, as we entered the supper-room; and to say the truth, fairy as she was, she made a remarkably good meal—consuming a couple of basins of white soup, several kinds of German sausages, some Westphalia ham, some white pudding, an anchovy-salad made with cornichons and onions, sweets innumerable, and a considerable quantity of old Steinwein and rum-punch afterwards. Then she got up and danced as brisk as a fairy; in which operation I, of course, did not follow her, but had the honour, at the close of the evening's amusement, once more to have her by my side in the sledge, as we swept in the moonlight over the snow. Kalsbraten is a very hospitable place as far as tea-parties are concerned, but I never was in one where dinners were so scarce. At the palace they occurred twice or thrice in a month; but on these occasions spinsters were not invited, and I seldom had the opportunity of seeing my Ottilia except at evening parties.

Nor are these, if the truth must be told, very much to my taste. Dancing I have foresworn, whist is too severe a study for me, and I do not like to play écarté with old ladies, who are sure to cheat you in the course of an evening's play.

But to have an occasional glance at Ottilia was enough; and many and many a napoleon did I lose to her Mamma, Madame de Schlippenschlopp, for the blest privilege of looking at her daughter. Many is the tea-party I went to, shivering into cold clothes after dinner (which is my abomination) in order to have one little look at the lady of my soul.

At these parties there were generally refreshments of a nature more substantial than mere tea—punch, both milk and rum, hot wine, consommé, and a peculiar and exceedingly disagreeable sandwich made of a mixture of cold white puddings and garlic, of which I have forgotten the name and always detested the savour.

Gradually the conviction came upon me that Ottilia ate a great deal.

I do not dislike to see a woman eat comfortably. I even think that an agreeable woman ought to be '*friande*,' and should love certain little dishes and knicknacks. I know that though at dinner they commonly take nothing, they have roast-mutton with the children at two, and laugh at their pretensions to starvation.

No! A woman who eats a grain of rice, like Amina in the 'Arabian Nights,' is absurd and unnatural; but there is a 'modus in rebus': there is no reason why she should be a ghoul, a monster, an ogress, a horrid gormandiseress—faugh!

It was then, with a rage amounting almost to agony, that I found Ottilia ate too much at every meal. She was always eating, and always eating too much. If I went there in the morning, there was the horrid familiar odour of those oniony sandwiches; if in the afternoon, dinner had been just removed, and I was choked by reeking reminiscences of roast-meat. Tea we have spoken of . . . She gobbled up more cakes than any six people present; then came the supper and the sandwiches again, and the egg-flip and the horrid rum-punch.

She was as thin as ever, paler if possible than ever:—but, by heavens! her nose began to grow red!

Mon Dieu! How I used to watch and watch it! Some days it was purple, some days had more of the vermilion

—I could take an affidavit that after a heavy night's supper it was more swollen, more red, than before.

I recollect one night when we were playing a round game (I had been looking at her nose very eagerly and sadly for some time), she of herself brought up the conversation about eating, and confessed that she had five meals a day.

'*That accounts for it!*' says I, flinging down the cards, and springing up and rushing like a madman out of the room. I rushed away into the night, and wrestled with my passion. 'What! Marry', said I, 'a woman who eats meat twenty-one times in a week, besides breakfast and tea. Marry a sarcophagus, a cannibal, a butcher's shop? —Away!' I strove and strove. I drank, I groaned, I wrestled and fought with my love—but it overcame me: one look of those eyes brought me to her feet again. I yielded myself up like a slave: I fawned and whined for her; I thought her nose was not so *very* red...

At this juncture the town of Hamburg sent his Highness the Grand Duke ... a singular present: no less than a certain number of barrels of oysters...

In honour of the oysters and the new commercial treaty ... his Highness announced a grand supper and ball, and invited all the quality of all the principalities round about. It was a splendid affair: the grand saloon brilliant with hundreds of uniforms and brilliant toilettes—not the least beautiful among them, I need not say, was Ottilia.

At midnight the supper-rooms were thrown open, and we formed into little parties of six, each having a table, nobly served with plate, a lacquey in attendance, and a gratifying ice-pail or two of champagne to *égayer* the supper. It was no small cost to serve five hundred people on silver, and the repast was certainly a princely and magnificent one. . .

The first course, of course, consisted of the *oysters*. Otillia's eyes gleamed with double brilliancy as the lacquey opened them. There were nine apiece for us—how well I recollect the number!

I never was much of an oyster-eater, nor can I relish them *in naturalibus* as some do, but require a quantity of sauces, lemons, cayenne peppers, bread and butter, and so forth, to render them palatable.

By the time I had made my preparations, Ottilia, the captains, and the two ladies, had well-nigh finished theirs. Indeed Ottilia had gobbled up all hers, and there were only mine left in the dish.

I took one—IT WAS BAD. The scent of it was enough—they were all bad. Ottilia had eaten nine bad oysters.

I put down the horrid shell. Her eyes glistened more and more; she could not take them off the tray.

'Dear Herr George,' she said, '*will you give me your oysters?*'

She had them all down—before—I could say—Jack—Robinson! . . .

I left Kalsbraten that night, and have never been there since.

THACKERAY, *Fitz-boodle's Confessions*.

V: FESTIVE SCENES

He hangs in shades the orange bright,
Like golden lamps in a green night,
And does in the pomegranates close
Jewels more rich than Ormus shows;
He makes the figs our mouths to meet,
And throws the melons at our feet;
But apples plants of such a price
No tree could ever bear them twice;
With cedars chosen by His hand,
From Lebanon he stores the land.

MARVELL.

BEING PART OF THE ENTERTAINMENT UNTO QUEEN ELIZABETH AT THE CASTLE OF KENILWORTH IN 1575

IT WAS EIGHT O'CLOCK in the evening e'er her Highness came to Kenilworth; where, in the Park, about a flight-shot from the Brase and first gate of the Castle, one of the ten Sybils comely clad in a pall of white silk pronounced a proper poesie in English rhyme and meter...

This, her Majestie benignly accepting, passed forth unto the next gate of the Brase... where the Lady of the Lake, with two Nymphs waiting upon her, arrayed all in silks attended her Highness's coming, from the midst of the Pool, where, upon a movable island, bright blazing with torches, she, floating to land, met her Majesty with a well-penned meter... This pageant was closed up with a delectable harmony of Hautbois, Shalms, Cornets, and such other loud music, that held on till her Majesty pleasantly so passed from thence toward the Castle gate, whereunto... was framed a fair Bridge... railed on either part with seven posts... Upon the first pair of posts were set two comely square wire cages... In them live Bitterns, Curlews, Shovellers, Herons... and such-like dainty Birds, of the presents of Sylvanus, the God of Fowls.

On the second pair, two great silvered bowls... filled with Apples, Pears, Cherries, Filberts, Walnuts, fresh upon their branches, and with Oranges, Pomegranates, Lemons, and Pippins, all for the gifts of Pomona, Goddess of Fruits. The third pair of posts, in two such silvered bowls, had (all in ears, green and gold), Wheat, Barley, Oats, Beans, and Peas, as the gifts of Ceres.

The fourth on the left hand, in a like silvered bowl, had Grapes in Clusters, white and red, graced by their Vine leaves. The corresponding post had a pair of great, white-silver livery pots, for wine, and before them, two glasses of good capacity, filled full, the ton with white Wine, the other two with Claret . . . and these for the potential presents of Bacchus, the God of Wine.

The fifth pair had each a large tray strewed a little with fresh grass, and in them Conger, Burt, Mullet, fresh Herring, Oysters, Salmon, Crayfish, and such like, from Neptune, God of the Sea. . .

Over the Castle gate was there fastened a Table beautifully garnished above with her Highness's arms, and featly with Ivy wreaths bordered about: of a ten foot square: the ground black, whereupon, in large, white, Roman Capitals, fair-written, a Poem mentioning these Gods, and their gifts thus presented unto her Highness...

Thus though the day took an end, yet slipt not the night all sleeping away. . . After supper was there a Play presented . . . after the Play followed a most delicious, if I may so term it, an Ambrosial, Banquet: whereof whether I might more muse at the daintiness, shapes, and the cost, or else at the variety and number of dishes, for my part I could little tell them, and now less I assure you. . . Unto this Banquet there was appointed a Mask, for riches of array of an incredible cost. . .

But the time so far spent . . . here I make an end: ye may breathe ye awhile.

Robert Laneham's Letter (Edited by Furnivall).

DINNER AT THE ROTHSCHILDS'

I DID NOT HEAR the announcement of *Madame est servie* without emotion. We proceeded to the dining-room, not as in England by the printed orders of the red-book, but by the law of the courtesy of nations, whose only distinctions are made in favour of the greatest strangers. The evening was extremely sultry, and in spite of Venetian blinds and open verandahs, the apartments through which we passed were exceedingly close. A dinner in the largest of them threatened much inconvenience from the heat; but on this score there was no ground for apprehension. The dining-room stood apart from the house, in the midst of orange trees: it was an elegant oblong pavilion of Greek marble, refreshed by fountains that shot in air through scintillating streams, and the table, covered with the beautiful and picturesque dessert, emitted no odour that was not in perfect conformity with the freshness of the scene and fervour of the season. No burnished gold reflected the glaring sunset, no brilliant silver dazzled the eyes; porcelain, beyond the price of all precious metals by its beauty and its fragility, every plate a picture, consorted with the general character of sumptuous simplicity which reigned over the whole, and showed how well the masters of the feats had consulted the genius of the place in all.

To do justice to the science and research of a dinner so served would require a knowledge of the art equal to that which produced it; its character, however, was, that it was in season—that it was up to its time—that it was in the spirit of the age—that there was no *perruque* in its composition, no trace of the wisdom of our ancestors in a single dish—no high-spiced sauces, no dark-brown gravies, no flavour of cayenne and allspice, no tincture of catsup and walnut pickle, no visible agency of those vulgar elements of cooking of the good old times, fire and water. Distillations of the most delicate viands, extracted in silver dews, with chemical precision—'on tepid clouds of rising steam'—formed the *fond* of all. EVERY MEAT PRESENTED ITS OWN NATURAL AROMA—EVERY VEGETABLE ITS OWN SHADE OF VERDURE: the *mayonnaise* was fried in ice (like Ninon's description of Sevigné's heart) and the tempered chill of the *plombière* (which held the place of the eternal *fondu* and *soufflées* of our English tables) anticipated the stronger shock, and broke it, of the exquisite *avalanche*, which with the hue and odour of fresh-gathered nectarines, satisfied every sense and dissipated every coarser flavour.

With less genius than went to the composition of this dinner, men have written epic poems; and if crowns were distributed to cooks, as to actors, the wreath of Pasta or Sontag (divine as they are) were never more fairly won than the laurel which should have graced the brow of Carème for this specimen of the intellectual perfection of an art, the standard and gauge of modern civilisation. Cruelty, violence and barbarism, were the characteristics of the men who fed upon the tough fibres of half-dressed oxen; humanity, knowledge, and refinement, belong to the living generation, whose tastes and temperance are regulated by the science of such philosophers as Carème, and such Amphitryons as his employers!

LADY MORGAN, *Letters*.

A PICNIC IN WESTMINSTER ABBEY

THE CORONATION of his present Majesty being fixed for the month of September, my father determined that all his family should be present at the ceremony. He therefore engaged one of the Nunnerys, as they are called, in Westminster Abbey, for which he paid fifty guineas. They are situated at the head of the great columns that support the roof and command an admirable view of the interior of the building. Upon this occasion they were divided off by wooden partitions, each having a separate entrance with lock and key to the door, with ease holding a dozen persons. Provisions, consisting of cold fowls, ham, tongues, different meat pies, wines and liquors of various sorts, were sent to the apartment the day before, and the two servants were allowed to attend. . .

We all supped together in St. Alban's Street on the 21st of September, and at midnight set off in my father's coach, and my Uncle's, and Miss Thomas's chariot. At the end of Pall Mall the different lines of carriages, nearly filling the street, our progress was consequently tedious, yet the time was beguiled by the grandeur of the scene, such a multitude of carriages, with servants behind carrying flambeaux, made a blaze of light equal to day, and had a fine effect. . .

It was half past seven in the morning before we reached the Abbey, which having once entered, we proceeded to our box without further impediment, Dr. Markam having given us tickets which allowed our passing by a private staircase, and avoiding the immense crowd that was within. We found a hot and comfortable breakfast ready, which I enjoyed, and which proved highly refreshing to us all; after which some of our party determined to take a nap in their chairs...

Their Majesties (the King having previously married) being crowned, the Archbishop of Canterbury mounted the pulpit to deliver his sermon, and, as many thousands were out of the possibility of hearing a single syllable, they took that opportunity to eat their meal, when the general clattering of knives, forks, plates, and glasses that ensued produced a most ridiculous effect, and a univeral burst of laughter followed.

HICKEY, *Memoirs*.

SUPPER IN A GROTTO AT STOWE

(*Horace Walpole to Madame du Deffand.*)

Strawberry Hill. Dimanche.

C'EST AVEC BEAUCOUP de satisfaction que je me retrouve chez moi... Malgré cette aversion pour le métier, j'ai fort bien joué mon rôle de courtisan; mais c'est que le terme était assez court. Nous nous sommes assemblés chez Milord Temple...

La maison est vaste, les jardins ont quatres milles de circonference, outre la forêt; des temples, des pyramides, des obelisques, des ponts, des eaux, des grottes, des statues, des cascades, voilà ce qui ne finit point. On dirait que deux ou trois empéreurs romains y eussent dépensés des trèsors... Milord Temple venait de faire bâtir un fort bel arc de pierre et de le dédier à la Princesse Cet arc est placé dans une orangerie, au sommet d'un endroit qu'on nomme les Champs-Elysées, et qui domine un très-riche paysage, au milieu duquel se voit un magnifique pont à colonnes, et plus haut la représentation d'un château à l'antique. La Princesse était dans les éxtases et visitait son arc quatre ou cinq fois par jours. Je m'avisai d'un petit compliment qui réussit à merveille! Autour de l'arc sont des statues d'Appollon et des Muses... Un jour la Princesse trouva dans la main du dieu des vers a sa louange...

On nous donna aussi un très joli amusement le soir. C'etait un petit souper froid dans une grotte au bout des Champs-Elysées, qui était éclairé par lampions dans des bosquets; et sur la rivière deux petits vaisseaux également ornés de lampions en pyramides... Mais en voilà assez; il ne faut pas vous ennuyer de nos promenades en cabriolet, de notre pharaon le soir, et de tous ces petits riens qui remplissent les moments à la campagne. Il suffit de dire que tout s'est passé sans nuages.

The Letters of Mme. du Deffand to Horace Walpole.

FASHIONABLE LONDON

AT THE TIME OF SWIFT, ADDISON AND STEELE

WHEN Lord Sparkish, Tom Neverout, and Colonel Allwit, the immortal personages of Swift's polite conversation, came to breakfast with my Lady Smart, at eleven o'clock in the morning, my Lord Smart was absent at the levée. His Lordship was at home to dinner at three o'clock to receive his guests; and we may sit down to this meal like the Barmecides's, and see the fops of the last century before us. Seven of them sat down at dinner, and were joined by a country baronet who told them they kept court hours. These persons of fashion began their dinner with a sirloin of beef, fish, a shoulder of veal, and a tongue. My Lady Smart carved the sirloin, my Lady Answerall helped the fish and the gallant Colonel cut the shoulder of veal. All made a considerable inroad on the sirloin and the shoulder of veal, with the exception of Sir John, who had no appetite, having already partaken of a beefsteak and two mugs of ale, besides a tankard of March beer as soon as he got out of bed. They drank claret, which the Master of the house said should always be drunk after fish; and my Lord Smart particularly recommended some excellent cider to my Lord Sparkish, which occasioned some brilliant remarks from that nobleman. When the host called for wine, he nodded to one or other of his guests, and said 'Tom Neverout, my service to you.'

After the first course came almond-pudding, fritters, which the Colonel took with his hands out of the dish, in order to help the brilliant Miss Notable; chickens, black puddings, and soup; and the Lady Smart, the elegant mistress of the mansion, finding a skewer in a dish, placed it in her plate, with directions that it should be carried down to the cook and dressed for the cook's own dinner. Wine and small beer were drunk during this second course; and when the Colonel called for beer, he called the butler Friend, and asked whether the beer was good. Various jocular remarks passed from the gentlefolk to the servants; at breakfast several persons had a word and a joke for Mrs. Betty, my lady's maid, who warmed the cream and had charge of the canister (the tea cost thirty shillings a pound in those days). When my Lady Sparkish sent her footman out to my Lady Match to come at six o'clock and play at quadrille, her ladyship warned the man to follow his nose, and if he fell by the way, not to stay to get up again. And when the gentleman asked the hall-porter if his lady was at home, that functionary replied, with manly waggishness, 'She was at home just now but she's not gone out yet.'

After the pudding, sweet and black, the fritters and soup, came the third course, of which the chief dish was a hot venison pasty, which was put before Lord Smart, and carved by that nobleman. Besides the pasty, there was a hare, a rabbit, some pigeons, partridge, a goose, and a ham. Beer and wine were freely imbibed during this course, the gentleman always pledging somebody, with every glass which they drank; and by this time the conversation between Tom Neverout and Miss Notable had grown so brisk and lively, that the Derbyshire baronet began to think the young gentlewoman was Tom's sweetheart; on which Miss remarked, that she loved Tom 'like pie.' After the goose, some of the gentleman took a dram of brandy, 'which was very good for the wholesomes,' Sir John said; and now having had a tolerably substantial dinner, honest Lord Smart bade the butler bring up the great tankard full of October to Sir John. The great tankard was passed from hand to hand and mouth to mouth, but when pressed by the noble host upon the gallant Tom Neverout, he said, 'No, faith, my lord, I like your wine, and won't put a churl upon a gentleman. Your honour's claret is good enough for me.' And so, the dinner over, the host said, 'Hang saving, bring us up a ha'porth of cheese . . .'

The cloth was now taken away, and a bottle of Burgundy was set down, of which the ladies were invited to partake before they went to their tea. When they withdrew, the gentlemen promised to join them in an hour: fresh bottles were brought; the 'dead men' meaning the empty bottles, removed; and 'd'you hear, John? bring clean glasses,' my lord Smart said. On which the gallant Colonel Allwit said, 'I'll keep my glass; for wine is the best liquor to wash glasses in.'

THACKERAY, *The Four Georges.*

A FOURTEENTH CENTURY BANQUET

THE boar's head shall be brought with bays aloft,
    Bucktails full broad in broths therewithal,
    Venison with the fruments, and pheasants full rich,
Baked meats near by, on the board well set,
Chewets of chopped flesh, and chickens grilled;
Each several guest has six men's share.
    Were this not enough, another course follows,
Roast with rich sauces and royal spice,
Kids cleft in the back, quartered swans,
Tarts of ten inches, it tortures my heart
To see the board o'er-spread with blazing dishes,
As a rood arrayed with rings and with stones.
    The third mess to me were a marvel to tell,
For all is Martinmass meat that I mostly know of,
Nought but worts with flesh-meat, without wild fowl,
Save a hen unto him that the house owneth;
And ye will have basted birds broach'd on a spit,
Barnacle-geese and bitterns, and many billed snipes,
Larks and linnets, lapp'd all in sugar,
Woodcocks and woodpeckers, full warm and hot,
Teals and titmice, to take what you please;
Caudels of conies, and custards sweet,
Dariols and dishmeats, that dearly cost,
Maumeny, as men call it, your maws to fill. . .

Winner and Waster (Edited by Gollancz).

AN ENGLISH AND A CHINESE DINNER

AFTER spending three very merry days at Whampoa, we returned to Canton where McClintock gave me a card of invitation to two different entertainments on following days, at the country house of one of the Hong merchants named Pankeequa. The fêtes were given on the first and second of October, the first of them being a dinner dressed and served *à la mode Anglaise*, the Chinamen on that occasion using, and awkwardly enough, knives and forks, and in every respect conforming to the European fashion. The best wines of all sorts were amply supplied. In the Evening a play was performed, the subject warlike, where most capital fighting was exhibited, with better dancing and music than I could have expected...

The second day on the contrary, everything was Chinese, all the European guests eating or endeavouring to eat, with chopsticks, no knives or forks being at table. The entertainment was splendid, the victuals extremely good, the Chinese loving high dishes and keeping the best of cooks. At night brilliant fireworks (in which they also excel) were let off in a garden magnificently lighted by coloured lamps which we viewed from a temporary building erected for the occasion, and wherein there was exhibited slight of hand tricks, tight and slack rope dancing, followed by one of the cleverest pantomimes I ever saw. This continued until a late hour, when we returned in company with several of the super cargoes to our factory, much gratified with the liberality displayed by our Chinese host.

HICKEY, *Memoirs*.

A BANQUET AT STRAWBERRY HILL

HORACE WALPOLE writes: 'Your poor beadsman, the Abbot of Strawberry, whose glories verge towards their setting, has been more sumptuous to-day than ordinary, and banqueted their representative majesties of France and Spain...

The refectory was never so crowded... A violent shower in the morning laid the dust, brightened the green, refreshed the roses, pinks, orange flowers, and the blossoms with which the acacias are covered. A rich storm of thunder and lightning gave a dignity of colouring to the heavens; and the sun appeared enough to illuminate the landscape, without basking himself over it at his length. During dinner there were French horns and clarionets in the cloister, and after coffee I treated them with an English, and to them very new collation—a syllabub milked under the cows, that were brought to the brow of the terrace. Thence they went to the printing house, and saw a new, fashionable French song printed. They drank tea in the gallery, and eight went away to Vauxhall. They really seemed quite pleased with the place and the day; but I must tell you, the treasury of the Abbey will feel it, for without magnificence, all was handsomely done.'

MELVILLE, *Horace Walpole*.

EXTRACTS FROM MISS BERRY'S JOURNAL 1802

FROM THE THEATRE came home, supped, changed our gowns, and between eleven and twelve went to the great ball given by M. Demidoff, a young Russian who has been here all the winter, and spending more than anybody... The house is in itself much ornamented, and was now decorated with much pink and silver drapery, and artificial flowers for the fête;... All the *jeunesse* of Paris were there of the new *régime*, and very many of the old... Vestris's figure was curious; his coiffure was one of those bustling, frizzed and powdered heads which were worn about twenty years ago, and in dancing, showers of powder came out of it, and it flapped up and down in the most ridiculous manner. M. de Lafitte was likewise frizzed and powdered, while the other two men, and indeed all the other men, wore crops. The women were in general well dressed, all *coiffées en cheveux* with flowers, and all the young ones dressed in white with bunches of flowers. In the antechamber was a *bouquetière*, who gave every lady as she entered a large bouquet of beautiful forced flowers, roses, carnations, etc., such as at Paris at this season could not cost less than twelve or eighteen livres apiece. These bouquets were changed as often as you pleased. The liveries of this Russian are more covered with gold lace than *anyone* ever saw *anywhere*, upon a *fond* of dark green and there were besides *chasseurs*, and *coureurs*, and *jockins*, and blacks, and little boys *habillés à la Tartare*, but all equally *gallonés* upon scarlet and black; and besides all this the persons who served (out of livery) were all in brown coats with a gold embroidery...

Supper was served as people desired it, and in any room where it was called for. To have the whole honour of this ball, Demidoff received himself, and did not allow his wife to do the honours.

Sunday 4th.

Went with Barrois to the Hameau de Chantilly, one of the many public gardens open most nights for dancing, etc. This was formerly the Hotel and garden of the Duchesse de Bourbon... It is extremely well laid out with many little intricacies, a large alley that goes round it, a broad terrace by the house, and a large sloping lawn before it. All this is well lighted with patent lamps, placed in large square glass lanterns hung across the walks and fixed in the bosquets and under the trees. Nothing can be prettier than both the general effect and the details of this garden. Under the trees was an excellent orchestra and there were, I know not how many, sets of French country dances. The dancers were *ouvrières*, mantua-makers, etc. In the intervals of the dancing they spread themselves about the garden, where at every step are placed little green tables with two or three chairs, and every here and there little rooms like cottages on the outside, and the lower part of the house is open.

All the gilding and painting upon the walls, and the glasses, remain just as they were in the time of Mme. de Bourbon; and in one of the rooms are still the fine tapestry *fauteuils* that originally belonged to the house; we were struck also with the locks and fastenings to the doors and windows being much handsomer than usual, and found that the arms of France were carefully obliterated from every one of them. All these rooms are well lighted and full of little tables and chairs, and here refreshments are to be had, with prices affixed to them in a long paper called *la carte*. But this is not all. The entry of this garden is 24 sous, of which 15 are allowed *en consommation* ... that is 15 sous worth of anything you please in food or in amusements; three country dances cost 5 sous apiece, or three turns of a *jeu de bague* or three courses upon the little lake, on which there are about a dozen little boats...

A large *salon* for dancing was arranged with *trèillage* paper, *trèillage* columns, and painted flowers and trees with the perspective of a garden and an avenue at the end, and green boxes for real flowers all round it, and a recess painted like a forest. Not the least remarkable part of this evening was that we were walking about at ten o'clock at night on the 4th of April and sitting in the open air without feeling cold, with the green buds all bursting over our heads, and the almond trees in full blow.

Tuesday, 22nd.

Soon after one o'clock went to call for Lady Charlotte Lindsay to go to Lady Buckinghamshire's *Venetian breakfast*. The house spacious, clean, and pretty, the garden looked pretty filled with young, and gaily-dressed people dancing, some of them in masks, many of them in dominoes, for this was the notion of a Venetian breakfast! The eating part of it was luckily quite *à l'Anglaise* good bread and butter, tea and coffee, etc.

Friday, March 22nd, 1811.

Went, about eleven, to Lady Hertford's. We did not get in till near twelve when the Regent had not arrived from dinner at Lord Cholmondeley's. He came soon afterwards while we were in the outer room, and we saw the whole ceremony. A circle was immediately made, and the Regent, the Dukes of Clarence, Cumberland, Cambridge, and Gloucester, were all in it at the same time. The Regent looked wretchedly, swollen up, with a muddled complexion, and was besides extremely tipsy—gravely and cautiously so. I happened to be a good while in the circle; and he at last gave me a formal grave bow, with *Kensington* legible on it.

In general he speaks much less both to men and women, than he did—it is the fashion of the day with him.

The Journals and Correspondence of Miss Berry.

DINNER WITH THE ABBOT OF ALCOBACA

IN CAME THE GRAND PRIORS hand in hand, all three together. 'To the kitchen,' said they in perfect unison, 'to the kitchen, and that immediately; you will then judge whether we have been wanting in zeal to regale you.' Such a summons, so conveyed, was irresistible; the three prelates led the way to, I verily believe, the most distinguished temple of gluttony in all Europe. What Glastonbury may have been in its palmy state, I cannot answer; but my eyes never beheld in any modern convent of France, Italy, or Germany, such an enormous space dedicated to culinary purposes. Through the centre of the immense and nobly groined hall, not less than sixty feet in diameter, ran a brisk rivulet of the clearest water, flowing through pierced wooden reservoirs, containing every sort and size of the finest river fish. On one side loads of game and venison were heaped up, on the other vegetables and fruit in endless variety. Beyond a line of stoves extended a row of ovens, and close to them hillocks of wheaten flour whiter than snow, rocks of sugar, jars of the finest oil, and pastry in vast abundance, which a numerous tribe of lay brothers and their attendants were rolling out and puffing up into an hundred different shapes, singing all the while as blithely as larks in a cornfield...

The banquet itself consisted of not only the most excellent usual fare, but rarities and delicacies of past seasons and distant countries; exquisite sausages, potted lampreys, strange messes from the Brazils, and others still stranger from China (edible birds' nests and sharks' fins) dressed after the latest mode of Macao by a Chinese lay brother... Confectionery and fruits were out of the question here; they awaited us in an adjoining, still more spacious apartment, to which we retired from the effluvia of viands and sauces... The table being removed, four good-looking novices, lads of fifteen or sixteen, demure even to primness, came in, bearing cassolettes of Goa filigree, steaming with a fragrant vapour of Calambac, the finest quality of wood of aloes.

Travel Diaries of William Beckford.

A RECEPTION AT GENJI'S PALACE

LATE in the tenth month the Emperor declared his intention of visiting Genji in the New Palace. Knowing that the maple leaves would be particularly lovely at this season, he invited the ex-Emperor Suzaku to accompany him...

The simultaneous reception of two such august visitors was a matter that required much forethought, and the dazzling preparations which Genji set afoot cost him hours of deliberation. The guests arrived at the hour of the Serpent. The first ceremony was a parade of the Bodyguards of the Right and Left, who lined up beside their horses exactly as at the Imperial Race-meeting in the fifth month. Early in the afternoon the Emperor proceeded to the Main Hall. All the plank bridges and galleries along which he passed were carpeted with costly brocades, and his progress was screened from the public gaze by heavy canvas curtains painted with landscape scenery. At the Eastern Lake the party embarked on boats, and the head cormorant-fisher from the Palace, combined with Genji's men, gave a display with his birds, who brought up a number of small gibel in their beaks. The fishing display was not part of the original programme, but was improvised at the last moment lest the royal personages should be bored on the way from the parade ground to the main Palace. Every knoll in the gardens was crowned by the scarlet of maple leaves...

The fish caught on the lake were to be submitted to the Emperor's approval by the Colonel of the Bodyguard of the Left. Meanwhile Genji's falconers returned from the Northern Fields with a string of birds which were handed over to the Colonel of the other Guard, who entering the Main Hall by the eastern doors, submitted the game kneeling at one side of the steps, while the fish were displayed on the other side. Tō no Chūjō, at his Majesty's command, directed the cooking of these viands, which were served to the Emperor himself, while the princes and noblemen in attendance were offered a repast of the most appetizing kind, in which every dish was served in a manner to some degree out of the ordinary. When everyone had had as much as he wanted, and dusk was setting in the musicians were sent for. It was not a formal concert, but there was some very lively dancing by various young pages from the Court. . . The professional musicians were not called upon to give any very exacting performance, and at an early hour the private playing began, led by the Emperor who sent to the Palace Library for a selection of zitherns. Prompted by the beauty of the season and the hour, one after another of the great personages there present called for his instrument and gave vent upon it to the feelings of the moment. Suzaku was deeply moved at hearing the familiar tones of Uda no Hōshi. Turning to the Emperor he recited the verse: 'Though, watcher of the woods, through many rainy autumns I have passed, such tints as these it never was my lot in any devious valley to behold.' The Emperor answered: 'You speak as though mere leaves were on the ground; here rather has autumn woven a brocade that, could it be an heirloom, after-ages would covet to possess.'

LADY MURASAKI, *Blue Trousers* (trans: by Waley).

FAME

THE SUN had set in glory over the broad expanse of waters still glowing in the dying beam; the people were assembled in thousands on the borders of the lake, in the centre of which was an island with a pavilion. Fanciful barges and gondolas of various shapes and colours were waiting for Lothair and his party, to carry them over to the pavilion, where they found a repast which became the hour and the scene: coffee and ices and whimsical drinks, which sultanas would sip in Arabian tales. No sooner were they seated than the sound of music was heard, distant, but now nearer, till there came floating on the lake, until it rested before the pavilion, a gigantic shell, larger than the building itself, but holding in its golden and opal seats Signor Mardoni and all his orchestra.

Then came a concert rare in itself, and ravishing in the rosy twilight; and in about half an hour, when the rosy twilight had subsided into a violet eve, and when the white moon that had only gleamed began to glitter, the colossal shell again moved on, and Lothair and his companions embarking once more in their gondolas, followed it in procession about the lake.

Suddenly a rocket rose with a hissing rush from the pavilion. It was instantly responded to from every quarter of the lake. Then the island seemed on fire, and the scene of their late festivity became a brilliant palace, with pediments and columns and statues, bright in the blaze of coloured flame. For half an hour the sky seemed covered with blue lights, and the bursting forms of many-coloured stars; golden fountains, like the eruption of a marine volcano, rose from different parts of the water; the statued palace on the island changed and became a forest glowing with green light; and finally a temple of cerulean tint, on which appeared in huge letters of prismatic colour the name of Lothair.

The people cheered, but even the voice of the people was overcome by troops of rockets rising from every quarter of the lake, and by the thunder of artillery. When the noise and the smoke had both subsided—the name of Lothair still legible on the temple but the letters quite white—it was perceived that on every height for fifty miles round they had fired a beacon.

DISRAELI, *Lothair*.

ENTREMETS

ENTREMETS in the middle ages were interludes, pantomimes, concerts, and even melodramas, performed before each course. In 1237 at the marriage of Robert, son of St. Louis, with Machault Countess of Artois, very singular spectacles were given between each course of the banquet. A horseman crossed the Hall by making his horse walk on a thick cord, extended above the heads of the guests. At the four corners of the table were musicians seated on oxen; and monkeys, mounted on goats, seemed to play the harp.

Among other amusements prepared for Queen Elizabeth, during her sojourn at the celebrated Castle of Kenilworth 'there was,' says Laneham, 'an Italian juggler, who performed feats of strength and leaps, and cut such capers with so much suppleness and ease, that I began to ask myself whether it were a man or a sprite.'

In England, during the Middle Ages, the Courts of Princes and Castles of the great were crowded with visitors who were always received with sumptuous hospitality. The pomp displayed by the lords was truly extraordinary... Troops of minstrels, clowns, jugglers, strolling players, rope-dancers, etc., lodged there at the great banqueting times. Each of the apartments open to the guests presented spectacles in harmony with the gross taste of the epoch. It was a marvellous confusion, a prodigious chaos, in which the ear was struck at once with the sound of dishes, of cups clasing one against another, of harmonious music, with the bustle of the dance, the notes of the song, pasquinades, somersaults, and everywhere the most boisterous laughter.

SOYER, *Pantropheon*.

A FÊTE FOR THE DUKE OF WELLINGTON

THE PRINCE'S personal tribute to Wellington took the form of a fête ... at Carlton House... The guests passed through the house into a great polygon structure, 120 feet in diameter, which had been erected in the gardens. This had been designed by the architect Nash, and was built of brick with a leaded roof. Inside it was entirely draped with white muslin, decorated with mirrors, and it had an umbrella-shaped roof painted to resemble muslin, so that the whole effect was extraordinarily light. In the centre of the room was a mass of artificial flowers in the shape of a temple, in which were concealed two bands... Leading from the west side of the polygon room, was a long covered walk decorated with muslin draperies, and ornamented with rose-coloured cords. This walk led to a Corinthian temple on the wall of which was a large mirror, over which was a brilliant star and the letter W cut in glass. On an antique column in front of the mirror was a marble bust of the Duke ... From this Corinthian temple opened out two supper tents, decorated with regimental colours in silk. Leading from the east side of the polygon room was a similar covered walk decorated in green calico. This walk was covered with allegorical transparencies, representing such subjects as, 'The overthrow of tyranny by the Allied Powers', 'Military Glory', and 'The Arts in England'...

After supper the Princess Mary, a spirited dancer of thirty-eight, opened the ball with the young Duke of Devonshire to the tune of 'Voulez-vous danser, Mademoiselle?'

FULFORD, *George IV*.

REGENCY FÊTES

AS SOON as the Prince was installed as Regent, he decided to give a fête at Carlton House to celebrate his accession to power... The supper table for the principal guests was 200 feet long and ran straight through the whole length of the Gothic conservatory and dining-room. The architecture of the conservatory, picked out with innumerable coloured lights placed in the niches, was set off to the best advantage. In the middle of the table, and raised six inches above it, flowed a stream of water supplied by a silver fountain, which played in front of the Prince. The banks of the stream were decorated with green moss and flowers, a few fanciful bridges were thrown across it, and gold and silver fishes swam in it...

One who was present wrote: 'The extraordinary part of it was, that so large a number should have been served in such a style; tureens, dishes, plates, even soup plates, were everywhere of silver with as many changes as were wanted. There were hot soups and roasts, all besides cold but of excellent and fresh cookery. Peaches, grapes, pine apples, and every other minor fruit in and out of season, were in profusion. Iced champagne at every three or four persons, all the other wines also excellent.'

The fête was only marred by one unfortunate incident. One of the most fashionable, but most ridiculous, figures in London society at that time was Mr. 'Romeo' Coates. He was a man of enormous wealth, with a particularly fine collection of diamonds. He used to drive about in a carriage shaped like a kettle drum and drawn by white horses: prominently displayed on the carriage was a large brazen cock, beneath which was his motto, 'While I live, I'll crow.'

To his surprise and intense gratification, he received an invitation to the Regent's fête. He spent days in the preparation of a magnificent suit, and he set out for Carlton House in excellent time, diamonds of the first water flashing on his bosom, his fingers, and his sword hilt. The crowd of onlookers gasped at the splendour of his servants' livery ...

He presented his card, but it was found to be a forgery, and this brilliant, dazzling figure was turned away. It was always thought to have been a practical joke of Sheridan's. When the Prince heard of it he was exceedingly annoyed that his servants should have pointed out the forgery, and the following day he sent his secretary to apologise to Mr. Coates and to invite him to come and see the decorations, which were still intact ...

There had been no rejoicings provided in which the crowd itself could join. This the Prince decided to remedy ...

Eastern architecture was at this time in complete possession of the Prince's mind, and a Chinese pagoda and bridge designed by Nash, were built across the lake in St. James's Park. The Green Park was reserved for fireworks, and there was much speculation as to the significance of a grim, Gothic, structure about 100 feet square, which had appeared there...

The public spectacle began with a balloon ascent from the Green Park by Mr. Sadler. This gentleman was the son of an eminent aeronaut, and, after working in the Liverpool Gas Company, was doubtless well qualified for his adventure ... A gallant lady called Mrs. Johnstone was to have accompanied the balloon, and she stood by it, clasping to her bosom a dove, which she was to have released from the heavens as an emblem of peace. At the last moment it was decided that the balloon was not safe for two: the ropes were cut, the balloon sprang into the air, and Mr. Sadler was last observed dropping favours from the sky. He was eventually found on the Essex coast, and only the judicious use of his knife in the bag of the balloon saved him from being carried out to sea ...

At eight a mimic naval battle, representing Trafalgar, began on the Serpentine ... and the greatest enthusiasm was aroused when the French fleet was finally destroyed by a fire ship. A profusion of fireworks of all kinds was fired from the battlements of the Gothic structure in the Green Park, after which the whole building was obliterated by smoke for two minutes. When the smoke had cleared, the Gothic fortress, which had only been canvas, had vanished, and in its place stood a Temple of Concord brilliantly illuminated ...

The Chinese pagoda on the bridge in St. James's Park was painted yellow, ornamented with black lines, and the roof painted bright blue. It was illuminated with gas and Japanese lanterns covered with glass reflectors... The fête was a memorable success... The credit for the fête. ... belongs primarily to the Prince... He was the ideal patron of victory. And as he watched from the windows of Buckingham House, and saw the rockets fizzing, the Chinese pagoda glittering with its gas lamps, the smoking Temple of Concord, the balloon sailing off on its perilous flight, and heard the shouts of the people and the hum of their enjoyment, he would have been less than human if he had not felt that he was in some way responsible for bringing the country to victory, and that the inscription on the Temple of Concord, 'The Triumph of England under the Regency', was not merely an empty compliment, but a sober demonstrable fact.

FULFORD, *George IV*.

A MOSCOW DINNER 1804

YESTERDAY we went at twelve o'clock to Count Ostrowman's... Immediately on entering we were led to a table where what is called a Breakfast was displayed—that is little odds and ends of dried fish, or Caviar, of Cheese, Bread, etc., and *eau de vie* were presented to us to give us an appetite for dinner which was announced almost immediately. We assembled in the Hall... surrounded by a sort of gallery which was filled with Men, Women, Dwarfs, children, Fools, and enraged musicians who sang and played with such powerful effect as to deafen those whom Heaven had spared...

A Trumpet sounded and 'blew a blast so loud and dread' that every tongue was silenced... A crystal vase filled with champagne was presented to the Master of the Castle. He stood up and quaffed the sparkling draught to the health of the Lady of the feast. The Trumpet sounded a second tune, the Goblet was presented to Princess Dashkaw who went thro' the same ceremony. A third time the Trumpet sounded and a third person quaffed from the same crystal vase to the same toast. In short the ceremony was repeated for every individual, and as there were a party of 46 you may judge the time which all the pomp and parade took up...

Many a bad dinner I made from the mere fatigue of being offered fifty or sixty different dishes by servants who come one after the other and flourish ready carv'd fish, flesh, fowl, Vegetables, fruits, soups of fish, etc., before your eyes, wines, Liqueures, etc., in their turn. Seriously the profusion is beyond anything I ever saw...

Yesterday we dined at Mr. Kissilof's where the only thing worth telling you about was a little Calmuck boy from the confines of China. He was brought in together with a little Circassian and an Indian to amuse the company, each dressed according to the fashion of his country. The two latter were not very remarkable, but the little Chineese was critically like the figures on old Indian screnes, cups and saucers, fans, etc... His dress was trousers of white Indian calico, a shawl served for shirt waistcoat, and all the rest of his dress, except a little spencer of scarlet cashimere edged with silver spangles... 'Tis here quite the custom to bring in men, or women or children, or fools, or anything that can entertain or amuse the company.

The Russian Journals of Martha and Catherine Wilmot
(Edited by Lady Londonderry).

A TRAINEAU PARTY
(*Moscow in* 1804)

AT a very agreeable sledging party ... which was given nominally for the Princess (Dashkaw) we were a few minutes late, and could scarcely gain admittance for the number of traineaus that were in the court and afterwards for the number of guests that were in the apartments. Soon after chocolate and cakes were handed, and then breakfast opened on our astonished optics in another room, which consisted of hot and cold soups, meat, fish, fowls, Ices, fruits, etc. The dessert was in another room, dry'd fruits, Cakes, and *eau de vie*. At length forty Traineaus, each drawn by six horses at least, quitted the House. In each Traineau were four people, two ladies and two gentlemen attended by two footmen and two or three postillions, etc. The *coup d'œuil* was superb. We drove like lightning round the Town ... each animating his coachman to unheard of exertions to pass the Traineau which was before him. ... We were dressed in all our best array; but don't figure to yourself fur caps, etc.—not at all—white satin on some, pink on others, etc.—black beaver on a few, and amongst that number was your humble servant. Shawls and pelisses protected us from the cold which, however, was not very intense that day. After parading with indefatigable speed for two hours and a half we returned to M. Kumberline's, arranged our Dresses as well as we could, drank tea, and then danced to conclude the evening.

The Russian Journals of Martha and Catherine Wilmot
(Edited by Lady Londonderry).

COFFEE IN A BAGNIO IN ADRIANOPLE

I WENT to the bagnio about ten o'clock. It was already full of women. It is built of stone, in the shape of a dome, with no windows but in the roof, which gives light enough. There were five of these domes joined together, the outmost being less than the rest and serving only as a hall... The next room is a very large one paved with marble, and all round it are two raised sofas of marble, one above another. There were four fountains of cold water in this room, falling first into marble basins and then running on the floor into little channels made for that purpose, which carried the streams into the next room—something less than this with the same sort of marble sofas, but so hot, with steams of sulphur proceeding from the baths joining to it, it was impossible to stay there with one's clothes on; the two other domes were the hot baths, one of which had cocks of cold water turning into it, to temper it to what degree of warmth the bathers pleased to have...

The first sofas were covered with cushions and rich carpets on which sat the ladies, and on the second their slaves, behind them, but without any distinction of rank by their dress, all being in the state of nature, that is, in plain English, stark naked, without any beauty or defect concealed. Yet there was not the least wanton smile or immodest gesture among them. They walked and moved with the same majestic grace which Milton describes our general Mother with. There were many amongst them as exactly proportioned as ever any goddess was drawn by the pencil of a Guido or a Titian—

most of their skins shiningly white, only adorned by their beautiful hair divided into many tresses hanging on their shoulders, braided either with pearls or ribbon, perfectly representing the figures of the Graces...

I was here convinced of the truth of a reflection I have often made—that if it were the fashion to go naked the face would be hardly observed. I perceived that the ladies of the most delicate skins and finest shapes had the greatest share of my admiration, though their faces were sometimes less beautiful than those of their companions. To tell you the truth I had wickedness enough to wish secretly that Mr. Jervas [a pupil of Kneller] could have been there invisible. I fancy it would have very much improved his art to see so many fine women naked in different postures, some in conversation, some working, others drinking coffee or sherbet, and many lying negligently on their cushions, while their slaves (generally pretty girls of seventeen or eighteen) were employed in braiding their hair in several pretty fancies. In short it is the women's coffee house, where all the news of the town is told, scandal invented, etc.

LADY MARY WORTLEY-MONTAGUE,
Letters.

LA FÊTE DE VERSAILLES

LA SCÈNE était à Versailles... Au milieu de l'étoile jaillissait une fontaine dont le bassin était environné de cinq tables sans nappes n'y couverts, où le naturel était si ingénieusement imité que, quelque splendide que fut la collation, elle y paraissait plûtot née que servie.

La première table était bornée, au bout qui tombait sur le bassin, par une montagne moussue, couverte de truffles et de champignons, ayant six entrées garnies de pâtés et de viandes froides, et le reste de la table, comme un fertile vallon, était jonché de salades et de verdures.

La seconde avait pareillement à l'un de ses bouts, comme en perspective, un corps d'architecture de différentes pâtés, et le reste était fourni de tourtes et d'autre pièces de four. La troisième était terminée par des pyramides de confitures sèches, et le reste de la table figuré comme un parterre régulier, par l'arrangement des massepains et des compôtes.

La quatrième semblait sortir d'un rocher escarpé, ou la nature avait commencé à former divers cristaux, et les restes de la table chargés de vases de crystal pleins de toutes sortes d'eaux glacées. La cinquième était bornée par des tas de caramels semblables à ces amas informes d'ambre que la mer pousse quelquefois au Rivage, et la table était couverte de porcelaines remplies de crèmes. Tout cela tenait plus de l'enchantement des fées que de l'industrie humaine. En effet, personne ne parut en ce lieu quand la compagnie y entra ; on entrevoyait seulement au travers des palissades des mains qui, sur des soucoupes très propres, présentaient à boire à tous ceux qui en voulaient...

La nuit cependant s'était beaucoup avancée... Sa Majesté convia la compagnie d'aller, à l'heure qu'il était, à l'autre côté du jardin, visiter une espèce de palais enchanté... Ses murs étaient tapissés en dehors d'un tissu de feuillages verdoyants... Huit portiques ds plus de quarante pieds de haut, et seize fenêtres ornées de festons, ouvraient de tous côtés un vaste salon de figure ronde; des pilastres, qui paraissaient de porphyre et dont les corniches étaient dorées, soutenaient un plafond à l'Italienne... Tout autour du salon, trois bassins en forme de coquilles elevées l'une sur l'autre, où l'eau formait diverses cascades, temperaient doucement le feu que jetaient des girandoles d'argent et plus de soixante lustres de crystal qui pendaient du plafond à differentes hauteurs... Au milieu des salons s'élevait un des rochers du Parnasse... Cet endroit, si vanté par les poètes, était environné d'une table à quatre-vingt couverts, éclairées de cents petits flambeaux de crystal et servie du plus grand souper du monde qui fut toujours egayé par la symphonie... Outre ces tables, qui n'étaient que pour les dames conviées, il y'en avait encore plusieurs autres dans diverses allées, où purent manger tous ceux qui en avaient envie, et dans la grotte, que vous savez être le plus bel endroit de Versailles, on avait dressé trois tables, pour régaler Messieurs les ambassadeurs... Je ne vous parlerai point de l'ordre, n'y de la pompe du bal, n'y de l'éclat, ni de la grâce de Leurs Majestés, de la beauté, ni de la parure des personnes qui dansèrent... L'aurore commençant à poindre sembla donner à tout le monde le signal de la retraite, et c'est, monsieur, ce qui couronna heureusement cette galante et magnifique fête.

ANON: 1668

VI: GASTRONOMIC INCIDENTS

To what would he on quail and pheasant swell
That ev'n on tripe and carrion could rebel?

DRYDEN.

A GREAT EPICURE

TWISTLETON FIENNES, the late Lord Saye and Sele... was a very eccentric man, and the greatest epicure of his day. His dinners were worthy of the days of Vitellius or Heliogabalus. Every country, every sea, was searched and ransacked to find some new delicacy for our British Sybarite. I remember, at one of his breakfasts, an omelette being served which was composed entirely of golden pheasants' eggs. He had a very strong constitution, and would drink absinth and curaçoa in quantities which were perfectly awful to behold. These stimulants produced no effect upon his brain; but his health gradually gave way under the excesses of all kinds in which he indulged. He was a kind, liberal, and good natured man, but a very odd fellow. I shall never forget the astonishment of a servant I had recommended to him. On entering his service, John made his appearance as Fiennes was going out to dinner, and asked his new master if he had any orders. He received the following answer—'Place two bottles of sherry by my bedside, and call me the day after to-morrow.'

GRONOW, *Reminiscences*.

'A PEACOCKE IS GREATER THAN AN APPLE'

HOLLINGSHED has given us a curious anecdote of Pope Julius III, that disgrace to the Romish See—an egregious glutton and epicure, whose favourite dish was the peacock:—'At another time he, sitting at dinner, pointing to a peacocke upon his table, which he had not touched, "Keepe," said he, "this cold peacocke for me against supper, and let me sup in the garden for I shall have ghestes." So when supper came and amongst the hot peacockes he saw not his cold peacocke brought to table, the Pope, after his wonted manner, most horribly blaspheming God, fell into an extreme rage. Whereupon one of his Cardinals sitting by him, desired him, saeing, "Let not your Holiness, I pray you, be so moved with a matter of so small weight." Then this Julius, the Pope, answering again, "What," said he, " if God was so angry for one apple, that he cast our first parents out of Paradise for the sinne, why may not I, being his vicar, be angry then for a peacocke, sithers a peacocke is greater than an apple."

Apician Morsels. Anon.

DES HUÎTRES TOUS LES MATINS

JE N'AI JAMAIS VU de lettre où il y'eût tant de bon sens que dans la vôtre; vous faites l'éloge de l'estomac si avanteusement qu'il y'aura de la honte à avoir bon esprit, à moins que d'avoir bon estomac. Je suis obligé à Monsieur l'Abbé Dubois de m'avoir fait valoir auprès de vous par ce bel endroit. A quatre-vingt ans, je mange des huîtres tous les matins, je dîne bien, je ne soupe pas mal; on fait des héros pour un moindre mérite que le mien.'

SAINT-EVRÉMONT, *Letter to Mlle. de Lanclos.*

VATEL'S TRAGEDY

(Mme. de Sevigné to Mme. de Grignan.)
Paris, Sunday, April 26th, 1671.

I HAVE JUST LEARNED from Moreuil of what passed at Chantilly with regard to poor Vatel. I wrote to you last Friday, that he had stabbed himself; these are the particulars of the affair. The King arrived there on Thursday night; the walk, and the collation, which was served in a place set apart for the purpose, and strewed with jonquils, were just as they should be. Supper was served, but there was no roast meat at one or two of the tables, on account of Vatel's having been obliged to provide several dinners more than were expected. This affected his spirits, and he was heard to say several times, 'I have lost my fame! I cannot bear this disgrace!' 'My head is quite bewildered,' said he to Gourville. 'I have not had a wink of sleep these twelve nights, I wish you would assist me in giving orders.' Gourville did all he could to comfort and assist him; but the failure of the roast meat (which, however, did not happen at the King's table, but at some of the other twenty-five) was always uppermost with him. Gourville mentioned it to the Prince, who went directly to Vatel's apartment, and said to him 'Everything is extremely well conducted, Vatel; nothing could be more admirable than His Majesty's supper.' 'Your Highness's goodness,' replied he, 'overwhelms me; I am sensible that there was a deficiency of roast meat at two tables.' 'Not at all,' said the Prince. 'Do not perplex yourself, and all will go well.' Midnight came: the fireworks did not succeed, they were covered with a thick cloud; they cost sixteen thousand francs. At four o'clock in the morning, Vatel went round, and found everybody asleep; he met one of the under-purveyors, who had just come in with only two loads of fish. 'What!' said he, 'is this all?' 'Yes, Sir,' said the man, not knowing that Vatel had dispatched other people to all the seaports round. Vatel waited for some time, the other purveyors did not arrive; his head grew distracted; he thought there was no more fish to be had; he flew to Gourville: 'Sir,' said he, 'I cannot outlive this disgrace.' Gourville laughed at him; Vatel, however, went to his apartment, and setting the hilt of his sword against the door, after two ineffectual attempts, succeeded in the third, in forcing the sword through his heart. At that instant the carriers arrived with the fish; Vatel was inquired after to distribute it; they ran to his apartment, knocked at the door, but received no answer; upon which they broke it open, and found him weltering in his blood. A messenger was immediately dispatched to acquaint the Prince with what had happened, who was like a man in despair. The Duke wept, for his journey to Burgundy depended upon Vatel. The Prince related the whole affair to His Majesty, with an expression of great concern: it was considered as the consequence of too nice a sense of honour; some blamed, others praised him for his courage. The King said he had put off this excursion for more than five years, because he was aware that it would be attended with infinite trouble, and told the Prince that he ought to have had but two tables, and not have been at the expense of so many, and declared he would never suffer him to do so again; but all this was too late for poor Vatel. However Gourville endeavoured to supply the loss of Vatel; which he did in great measure.

MME. DE SEVIGNÉ, *Lettres*.

TRUFFES À LA PURÉE

IT IS RELATED of Herbault, of bonnet-making fame, that when he was occupied with the more recondite mysteries of his art, his porter was wont to put off visitors with, 'Monsieur n'est pas visible, il compose.' When the Duc D'Escars and his royal master were closeted together to meditate a dish, the ministers were kept waiting in the antechamber, and the next day the following announcement appeared in the official journals: 'Monsieur le Duc d'Escars a travaillé dans le cabinet.' Louis XVIII had invented the *truffes à la purée d'ortolans*, and reluctant to disclose the secret to an ignoble confidant or menial, he invariably prepared the dish with his own royal hands, assisted by the Duc. On one occasion they had jointly composed a dish of more than ordinary dimensions, and duly consumed the whole of it. In the middle of the night the Duc was seized with a fit of indigestion, and his case was declared hopeless: loyal to the last, he ordered an attendant to wake and inform the King, who might be exposed to a similar attack. His Majesty was roused accordingly, and told that his faithful servant was dying of his invention. 'Dying!' exclaimed Louis le Desiré—dying of my *truffes à la purée*? I was right then, I always said I had the better stomach of the two.'

The Art of Dining. Anon.

A CHEF

THE DUKE OF WELLINGTON once requested the connoisseur whom the author of Tancred terms the finest judge in Europe, to provide him a chef. Felix, whom the late Lord Seaford was reluctantly about to part with on economical grounds, was recommended and received. Some months afterwards, his patron was dining with Lord Seaford, and before the first course was over he observed, 'So I find you have got the Duke's cook to dress your dinner.' 'I have got Felix,' replied Lord S., 'but he is no longer the Duke's cook. The poor fellow came to me with tears in his eyes and begged me to take him back again, at reduced wages or no wages at all, for he was determined not to remain at Apsley House. "Has the Duke been finding fault?" said I. "Oh! no, my Lord, I would stay if he had: he is the kindest and most liberal of masters; but I serve him a dinner that would make Ude or Francatelli burst with envy, and he says nothing; I serve him a dinner dressed and badly dressed, by the cookmaid, and he says nothing. I cannot live with such a master, if he was a hundred times a hero." '

The Art of Dining. Anon.

AN ANECDOTE

AN ANECDOTE (related to Colonel Damer by Talleyrand) may help to rescue the fair fame of Brillat-Savarin from the reproach of indifference and illustrate the hereditary quality of taste. He was on his way to Lyons, and was determined to dine at Sens. On his arrival he sent, according to his invariable custom, for the cook, and asked what he could have for dinner? The report was dispiriting. 'Little enough,' was the reply. 'But let us see,' retorted M. Savarin, 'let us go to the kitchen and talk the matter over.' In the kitchen he found four turkeys roasting. 'Why!' exclaimed he, 'You told me you had nothing in the house. Let me have one of these turkeys.' 'Impossible!' said the cook, 'they are all bespoken by a gentleman upstairs.' 'He must have a large party to dine with him then?' 'No, he dines by himself.' 'I should like much to be acquainted with the man who orders four turkeys for his own eating.' The cook was sure that the gentleman would be glad of his acquaintance; and M. Brillat-Savarin immediately paid his respects to the stranger, who turned out to be his own son. 'What, you rogue, four turkeys, all for yourself?' 'Yes, Sir, you know that whenever I dine with you you eat up the whole of *les sots les laissent*'—the tit-bit which we call the *oyster* of the turkey or fowl—'I was resolved to enjoy myself for once in my life, and here I am ready to begin, although I did not expect the honour of your company.'

The Art of Dining. Anon.

A BET

I WON a small bet from Lady Diana Beauclerk, by asking him—Johnson—as to one of his particularities, which her Ladyship laid I durst not do. It seems he had been frequently observed at the Club to put into his pocket the Seville oranges, after he had squeezed the juice of them into the drink which he made for himself. Beauclerk and Garrick talked of it to me, and seemed to think that he had a strange unwillingness to be discovered. We could not divine what he did with them; and this was the bold question to be put. I saw on his table the spoils of the preceding night, some fresh peels nicely scraped and cut into pieces. 'Oh, Sir,' said I, 'I now partly see what you do with the squeezed oranges which you put into your pocket at the Club.'

Johnson: 'I have a great love for them.'

Boswell: 'And pray, Sir, what do you do with them? You scrape them it seems, very neatly, and what next?'

Johnson: 'Let them dry, Sir.'

Boswell: 'And what next?'

Johnson: 'Nay, Sir, you shall know their fate no further.'

Boswell: 'Then the world must be left in the dark. It must be said (assuming a mock solemnity) he scraped them, and let them dry, but what he did with them next he never could be prevailed upon to tell.'

Johnson: 'Nay, Sir, you should say it more emphatically:—He could not be prevailed upon even by his dearest friends to tell.'

BOSWELL, *Life of Samuel Johnson.*

THE LION'S SHARE

DOCTOR GEORGE FORDYCE, the great anatomist and chemical lecturer, resembled Professor Porson in the strength and length of his libations, nor was he less remarkable for his powers of absorbing food. A great admirer of the lion, his studies in comparative anatomy had brought him to conclude that this sagacious animal is the wisest eater; for he eats but once a day, and then as much as nature will permit. So for twenty years Dr. Fordyce followed the same régime as the object of his admiration, although, as we shall see, he did not confine himself to drinking water. Every day at four o'clock he would enter Dolly's Chop House ... and immediately on his arrival the cook would put a pound and a half of rump steak on the gridiron, whilst the waiter brought the professor some hors d'œuvre, in the shape of half a broiled chicken or a large plate of fish, together with a silver tankard of strong ale, a bottle of port and a quarter of a pint of brandy. All these vanished in the twinkling of an eye, for the Doctor, like the lion, did not toy with his food or his drink—he ate and he drank as if he were performing a race for a bet. Having finished his meal, he then made his way to the Chapter Coffee House ... where he drank a glass of brandy and water, a second glass was provided at the London Coffee House, and a third at the Oxford, after which the Professor, considerably refreshed, returned to his house ... and thundered out his lectures on Chemistry. Nor did he eat again until at 4 o'clock on the following day he returned to Dolly's.

This habit, however, led to strange results at moments; and on one occasion, when Dr. Fordyce attended a lady who had been stricken with illness of a sudden and mysterious nature, he found he was unable to count the beats of her pulse. This, indeed, seemed to have discovered the secret of perpetual motion, whirling madly round and round in one direction, whilst Dr. Fordyce's brain persisted in whirling equally madly in the contrary sense. Irritated by this phenomenon, but tracing it to its source in Dolly's Chop House, the Professor ejaculated: 'Drunk, by the Lord!' Rather to Dr. Fordyce's surprise the lady wept silently, and Dr. Fordyce, having prescribed some remedy, left the room with dignity and precision. Next day he received a message begging for an immediate interview with him, and as soon as he arrived the lady, bursting into tears, confessed that he had diagnosed her illness only too correctly. The reproof administered by the Professor was severe in the extreme, and the lady promised that there should be no recurrence of the malady.

EDITH SITWELL, *The English Eccentrics*.

BYRON'S DINNER WITH ROGERS

NEITHER Moore nor myself had ever seen Byron when it was settled that he should dine at my house... When we sat down to dinner I asked Byron if he would take soup? 'No, he never took soup.'—'Would he take fish?' 'No, he never took fish.' —Presently I asked if he would eat some mutton? 'No, he never ate mutton.'—I then asked if he would take a glass of wine? 'No, he never tasted wine.'—It was now necessary to inquire what he *did* eat and drink; and the answer was, 'Nothing but hard biscuits and soda-water.' Unfortunately, neither hard biscuits nor soda-water were at hand; and he dined upon potatoes bruised down on his plate and drenched with vinegar.—My guests stayed till very late discussing the merits of Walter Scott and Joanna Baillie.—Some days after, meeting Hobhouse, I said to him, 'How long will Lord Byron persevere in his present diet?' He replied, 'Just as long as you continue to notice it.' I did not then know, what I now know to be a fact—that Byron, after leaving my house, had gone to a Club in St. James's Street, and eaten a hearty meat-supper.

ROGERS, *Table Talk*.

AN ECONOMICAL DINNER

ONE DAY, when some friends were expected to dine with Mrs. Nollekens, poor Bronze, labouring under a severe sore-throat, stretching her flannelled neck up to her mistress, hoarsely announced '*all the Hawkinses*' to be in the dining-parlour! Mrs. Nollekens, in a half-stifled whisper, cried 'Nolly! It is truly vexatious that we are always served so when we dress a joint: you won't be so silly as to ask them to dinner?' *Nollekens*. 'I ask them! Let 'em get their meals at home; I'll not encourage this sort of thing; or, if they please, they can go to the Mathias's, they'll find the cold leg of lamb we left yesterday!' ... Shortly after, the invited party arrived... In the meantime, Bronze, who had been assisting the cook to put on the dishes, called to me through the keyhole, 'Bless you! Master Smith, come and see our set-out!' and as the scanty display for so many persons astonished me, I shall endeavour to describe the 'spread' as it is called at Cambridge. Two tables were found; but as the legs of one were considerably shorter than those of the other, four blocks of wood had been prepared to receive them. The damask tablecloth was of a coffee-colour, similar to that formerly preferred by washers of court-ruffles. I recollect that the knives and forks matched pretty well; but the plates of Queen's ware had not only been ill-used by being put upon the hob, by which they had lost some of their gadrooned edges, but were of an unequal size, and the dishes were flat, and therefore held little gravy. The dinner consisted of a roasted leg of pork, the joint scented by their friend Taylor; a salad with four heads of celery standing pyramidically; mashed turnips neatly spooned over a large plate to the height of a quarter of an inch; and lastly,

> *Lo! a lobster introduced in state*
> *Whose ample body stretches o'er the plate.*

The side dishes were a chicken and a reindeer's tongue, with parsley and butter, but the boat was without a ladle, and the plate hardly large enough for it to stand in. Close to Mrs. Nolleken's left elbow, stood a dumb-waiter with cheese, a slice of butter, a few water-cresses, and a change of plates, knives and forks.

The dinner being announced, there was a great rustling of silks for preference of places, and I concluded, by the party drawing their chairs close, they were ready to begin; but Bronze used to say, 'No-one could eat till he was red in the face at master's table.' The set at the table consisted of Nolleken, his wife, and five on a side. No challenge at dinner that I heard of, nor do I think wine was ever mentioned until the servants were ordered to '*take off*.' Much about this time I distinctly heard Mrs. Nolleken's voice vociferate, 'I will have it found!' At last Bronze entered, to whom she had given peremptory commands to fetch it. *Mr. Nolleken*: 'And *arter* all, pray where did you find it?' *Bronze*: 'Why, Sir, under the pillow of your bed.'—'There, Mr. Nolleken, I knew you had used it last night.' Nolleken ordered Bronze out of the room, saying, 'he never liked that woman—her mouth looked like the rump of a chicken.' This nameless article was then caught first by one elderly maiden and then by another; and as for Miss Welch, she declared a '*back-scratch*' to be the most agreeable thing imaginable.

J. T. SMITH, *Nollekens and his Times*.

JOHNSON ON THE FRENCH

THE FRENCH are an indelicate people, they will spit upon any place. At Madame du Boccage's, a literary lady of rank, the footman took the sugar in his fingers and threw it into my coffee. I was going to put it aside, but hearing it was made on purpose for me, I e'en tasted Tom's fingers. The same lady would needs make tea *à l'Anglaise*. The spout of the tea-pot did not pour freely; she bade the footman blow into it. France is worse than Scotland in everything but climate. Nature has done more for the French, but they have done less for themselves than the Scotch.

BOSWELL, *Life of Samuel Johnson*.

SWIFT'S HOSPITALITY

POPE described to Spence one occasion when he and Gay paid an unexpected visit to the Dean. 'On our coming in: "Hey-day, gentlemen," says the Doctor, "what's the meaning of this visit? How came you to leave all the great lords that you are so fond of, to come hither to see a poor Dean?"

"Because we would rather see you than any of them."

"Ay, ay, one that did not know you so well as I do might believe you. But since you are come I must get some supper for you I suppose?"

"No, Doctor, we have supped already."

"Supped already? that's impossible, why 'tis not eight o'clock yet."

"Indeed, we have."

"That's very strange. But if you had not supped I must have got something for you. Let me see, what should I have had! A couple of lobsters? Ay, that would have done very well: two shillings: tarts, a shilling. But you will drink a glass of wine with me, though you supped so much before your usual time only to spare my pocket?"

"No, we had rather talk with you than drink with you."

"But if you had supped with me, as in all reason you ought to have done, you must have drunk with me—a bottle of wine, two shillings—two and two is four, and one is five; just two and sixpence apiece. There, Pope, there's half a crown for you; and there's another for you, Sir; for I won't save anything from you, I'm determined."

'This was all said and done with his usual seriousness on such occasions; and in spite of everything we could say to the contrary, he actually obliged us to take the money.'

EDITH SITWELL, *Alexander Pope.*